Fred,

May God continue to
bless you and keep you in his

peace.

HEBRAIC CHRISTIAN
GLOBAL COMMUNITY™

Understanding the Jewish roots of our faith is a golden key that unlocks the treasures of Holy Scripture and enriches Christian lives. This fundamental concept is the focus of Hebraic Christian Global Community, an international, trans-denominational, multicultural publishing and educational resource for Christians.

Hebraic Christian Global Community features individuals and congregations who share the vision for restoring Christianity's Hebraic foundations, for networking together in true community, and for returning the church to a biblical relationship of loving support for the international Jewish community and the nation of Israel.

We publish **Restore!** magazine, a high-quality journal featuring theological balance and scholarly documentation that helps Christians recover their Hebrew heritage while strengthening their faith in Jesus.

We also publish **Hebraic Insight**, a quarterly Bible-study journal that assists individuals, families, study groups, and congregations in inductive Hebraic study of the Scriptures that is accurate, balanced, and trustworthy.

We also distribute books from **Golden Key Press** in order to disseminate high quality teaching about Christianity's Hebraic foundations that is non-threatening and non-judgmental and helps believers grow in Christian understanding.

We also provide various media resources through **New Treasures** media productions. Many of these can be accessed on our website.

The ministry of Hebraic Christian Global Community is made possible by our many partners around the world who share in our **Golden Key Partnership** program. We invite you to join us in sharing the satisfaction of knowing that you are a partner in an organization that is making a difference in the world by restoring Christians to their biblically Hebraic heritage, by eradicating Judaeophobia and anti-Semitism, by supporting Israel and the international Jewish community, and by encouraging collaborative efforts among those who share this vision.

For information about Hebraic Christian Global Community and all our resources and services, contact us at:

Hebraic Christian Global Community
P. O. Box 421218
Atlanta, Georgia 30342, U.S.A.
www.HebraicCommunity.org

Family Worship

Making Your Home a
House of God

Family Worship: Making Your Home a House of God

Unless otherwise noted, Scriptuyre quotations are from the New American Standard Bible.

Cover design by Resolute Creative, Houston, TX

First Edition
Published by Golden Key Press, Atlanta, GA

This book is printed on acid-free paper that meets the American National Standards Institute Z39.48 standard.

ISBN
Library of Congress Control Number: 2013937143

Library of Congress Cataloging-in-Publication Data

Garr, John D.
        Family Worship / John D. Garr. -1st ed. p. cm.
        Includes index.
        ISBN 978-0-9794514-7-8
        1. Doctrinal Theology. 2. The Bible. 3. Christianity. 5. Judaism. 6. The Family, Marriage, Women, Men . I Title BT695-749

Family Worship

Making Your Home
a House of God

John D. Garr, Ph.D.

Hebraic Christian Global Community
P. O. Box 421218
Atlanta, Georgia 30342, U.S.A.

To our loyal friends and colleagues
Roland and Janis Leal
and their children, Emilie, Elise, Caroline,
Abigail, Luke, Ava, Josiah, Caleb, Eden, and
Ella—who together epitomize the biblically
Hebraic family temple ideal.

TABLE OF CONTENTS

Introduction

Everyone needs sanctuary, a place of peace and safety, a place of blessing and affirmation, a place of sanctity and security, a place of social and spiritual development, and a place of learning and personal growth. These are some of the specific functions for which God designed the home from time immemorial. God himself was the creator of family and the home, and what he created works. When people simply follow his instructions, determining to do God's thing God's way, the outcome is inevitable and amazingly good!

Through the centuries, however, persistent and unrelenting attacks have been made upon the family, the most fundamental unit of both societies and worshipping communities. Hellenization, Latinization, and secularization have rendered the modern Christian home a mere shadow of what it was in biblical times. Profoundly important elements of God's design for human relationships have been jettisoned in favor of human ideas and opinions. Today, both marriage and family are continually being redefined by societies bent on accommodating virtually every perversion that the human heart can imagine, all in the name of equality and tolerance.

God's design for the home, however, has always been and will always be the same. It becomes perfectly clear when we carefully examine the biblical record and then determine to return the family and home to the matrix from which it emerged. It is not enough, however, to call simply for "biblical" restoration. The term *biblical* has become so diluted that it has been virtually eviscerated of meaning. Almost every organization in Christianity considers its beliefs, teachings, and practices to be "biblical," and everyone knows that the myriads of ideas and applications that are called "biblical" cannot possibly be biblical. The unfortunate truth about most faiths in today's world is that they *claim* to be biblical but they fall far short of *being* biblical.

The problem is that practically all societies and people groups have read their own concepts and cultures into the Bible rather than drawing out from the Holy Scriptures the truths that have always been there. The church's approach to the Holy Writ has been ignorant at best and disingenuous at worst. When interpreting the Bible, Christians have engaged in eisegesis rather than exegesis by injecting their preconceived notions into Scripture rather than extracting from the text what it clearly says.

Texts without contexts have become pretexts for proof texts! The grammar of the Scriptures (the Hebrew language of the first testament and the Hebrew thought underlying the Greek language of the second testament) has been largely minimized if not downright ignored. Likewise, the history and culture of the people through whom and to whom the sacred texts were committed have been virtually ignored. Entire theologies have been based upon a "criterion of dissimilarity" in which texts in the Apostolic Scriptures that have clear connections with the Hebrew Scriptures have been dismissed by some scholars as not being the authentic words of Jesus and the apostles but the work of subsequent redactors. It is as though Jesus had to have been born and lived in a vacuum and never influenced by his native language and culture. The very idea has given rise to a Christianity that has been wrenched from its theological and historical moorings and set adrift in a maelstrom of nonbiblical—in far too many cases, anti-biblical—traditions, including postmodernism, consequentialism, secular humanism, and even demonic perversion.

It is not enough, therefore, to be simply biblical, for the Scriptures can be and have been wrested and used to support clearly nonbiblical ideas and practices. In order to restore society to a "biblical" basis, the church must first restore the Hebraic roots of the Christian faith. It is time for a full recovery of the sixteenth-century Reformation Hermeneutic (a set of rules for interpreting Scripture) by affirming and practicing the grammatico-historical method: considering the Hebrew grammar of the texts themselves (including the underlying Hebrew thought of the Greek texts of Apostolic Scriptures) and the history and culture of the Hebrew peoples to whom and through whom God disclosed the revelation that became Holy Scripture.

In order for true biblical order to be restored, a return to the "biblically Hebraic" must take place. This will require much focus and determination, for the Greco-Roman worldview and mindset have been forced upon the Scriptures for so many centuries that in many cases the Scriptures themselves have become almost unrecognizable in popular "interpretations." In other words, "back to the Bible" means back to Hebraic thought and practice. This is especially true in the important arena of human relationships. God's perspectives on family and the home can never be understood without a renewal of the Hebraic truths which God himself established as the foundation for this core element of human existence.

A complete rethinking of the issues of family and home is, therefore, not only desirable; it is absolutely essential. Church traditions founded in Greek philosophy and in various polytheistic and monistic religions must be completely abandoned. If today's society is to be saved from implosion because of the destruction of its nuclear unit (the family), a return to biblically Hebraic understanding must become top priority. Nothing short of a restoration of Hebraic truth will suffice.

God's Word works! What God has said will outlast everything that exists. "Heaven and earth will pass away, but my words will never pass away," Jesus declared in Mark 13:31. What God said about family and home is ultimate truth, and God's Word is the only thing that will endure. Since God dynamically modeled his instructions regarding society's fundamental unit among the Jewish people, it is to the Jewish people and to the Hebrew Scriptures that the church and society must look for understanding that will renew the biblical family and bring health and vitality to society at large.

Trying to fabricate a program that will somehow accommodate the modern notion of family by obliquely incorporating biblical terminology into postmodern philosophical, sociological, or psychological categories will only result in furthering the disaster. A thin veneer of religiosity over politically correct societal definitions of family will not suffice. Likewise, any attempt to syncretize biblical thought with postmodern secular theories is destined to utter failure.

It is for this reason that I have undertaken to write this volume. I believe that recovering the Hebraic foundations of the Christian faith is a golden key that unlocks the treasures of Holy Scripture and brings to the lives of believers the enrichment that only divine truth can bring. Hebraic truth is the mainstay of all things biblical. In no area of life could this be more true than in consideration of the dynamics of family and the home.

I wish to thank my faithful colleague, Dr. Karl Coke, for his continuing insightful teaching on the primacy and centrality of the family as the institution for spiritual growth and maturity for Christian believers. My colleagues, Dr. Marvin Wilson and Dwight Pryor (of blessed memory) have also contributed superb teaching to the body of Messiah and to my understanding on this important issue. Judy Grehan has also been an invaluable asset with her thoughtful observations and careful copy editing of this book.

A host of other friends have joined together with Pat and me as an extended family in community, lending their support, prayers, and advice as we seek to provide quality, theologically sound, and conceptually balanced materials on which individuals and faith communities can build successful lives and ministries. It is a challenge that we do not take lightly, nor do we imagine in our wildest dreams that we could do it alone. The network of scholars and leaders with whom we are laterally connected gives us mutual accountability both academically and spiritually, and for that we are exceedingly grateful.

I believe that as you read this volume, you will be challenged to consider new insights on what I believe to be rock-solid biblical and historical positions on some of the most important issues in life, those that impact the family and the home. In today's world of rabid postmodern pluralism, this is radical thought, but it is radical in the truest sense of the word *radical*, which means "going to the root or origin" (from the Latin *radix* meaning "a root"). Returning to the Jewish roots of your Christian faith may seem radical and a bit disconcerting. It may be challenging and formidable, but it will also be rewarding and fulfilling.

Transforming your home into a house of God may, indeed, represent a profound paradigm shift for you and for your loved ones; however, doing God's thing God's way will always work, and it will bring joy and peace into your home that you never imagined possible. You may well be stretched, but you must always remember that it is stretching that produces both strength and flexibility, qualities that you and your family will need in order to survive the challenges of today's inhospitable world.

To the end that you will be strengthened in the most holy faith I pray that my analysis of Scripture and history will assist you in establishing and maintaining the sanctity of your family circle and that it will empower you to transform your home into a house of God, a true center for family worship.

Fraternally in Messiah
John D. Garr, Ph.D.
Passover, 2013

Chapter 1

Society's Heart and Soul

THE INDISPENSABLE FAMILY

Home! A respite of safety and security. Repose in loving, affirming relationships. Relief from stress and rest from labor. A retreat to sanity from a world of madness. An oasis of peace in an angry, troubled, and threatening realm of human failure. A refuge for spiritual renewal, growth, and development. The biblically Hebraic home is God's provision for all of this and more! Indeed, the very sound of the word *home* speaks rest to a troubled, weary soul. It's a sigh of relief for the harried and well-traveled. It's a profound exhale from the pent-up stress of life's often cruel demands. This is the idea of the home that is centered in traditions outlined in the Holy Scriptures.

"Homes are central to our lives," say Baruch HaLevi and Ellen Frankel. "Our home is where we spend most of our time, form our deepest relationships, our identity, and where the [Spirit] most fully comes into our lives."[1] Unfortunately, however, this is not a description of the average home in dysfunctional Western culture. During the past few decades, revisionist attempts have been made to redefine both the family and the home. People with political agendas designed on societal or world domination have made savage efforts to restructure the understanding of the home or to destroy it altogether. The biblical ideal of the nuclear family has been under heavy attack from demonic societal forces intent upon its destruction.[2]

Still, family remains the fundamental building block of society, and the home is society's heart and soul. Healthy homes produce healthy societies. When societies have strong and mutually affirming bonds in the home, a general sense of security provides an atmosphere conducive to personal growth and the resultant courage to strive for excellence. On the other hand, when the bonds of family are not valued and strengthened, a general sense of insecurity arises, resulting in malaise and irresponsibility. Dysfunctional homes produce societies marked by either anarchy or autocracy. Without the safety and security that family boundaries provide, the selfishness of the human heart leaps to the fore in unmentionable acts of violence and moral depravity. When societies depart from the fundamental model of social interaction that the Creator designed the family to be, fundamental standards for morality disappear, and general societal disintegration becomes inevitable.

DYSFUNCTIONALITY AND DEMOLITION

The mad and maddening quest for "success" that has glorified—even deified—individual accomplishment in the modern and postmodern worlds has left many, if not most, homes hollow shells, void of any resemblance to the family of ancient times. An egocentric generation has reduced the home to little more than an overnight rest stop for strangers. The family table (*qua* snack bar or merely refrigerator) has become little more than a feeding station for increasingly restless generations on the move.

The assertion that every want and whim must somehow be an inalienable right has fertilized the growth of perhaps history's most selfish generation. The "have-it-your-way" mentality has been so reinforced by clever advertising which is so pervasive that even chest-thumping popular songs boast, "I did it my way." Parents are so acclimated to demanding their own individual rights that they give little thought to sacrificing in order to maintain a secure family environment. Many are so consumed with self-love that any thought of love as sacrifice is anathema.

This is an emotionally stimulated generation that wants to be free to feel, not to think. Because everything is assigned value on the basis of either feeling or utility, everything is consequently devalued. The music industry has become a diabolical medium for disseminating hate, violence, promiscuity, and perversion. The more vile the performance, the more admired and imitated the idol. "Reality Television" has glamorized the dregs of society, convincing young people that the way to instant fame and fortune is to have no talent—to know nothing, do nothing, and be nothing but a narcissistic exhibitionist. The result is that in much of Western society today, alley-cat morality is glamorized, and canine mores are the norm. And, after all, since humanism, the "religion" of agnostic, secularist society, says that all humans are the product of evolution, why would people not want to act like animals? This is why children of the MTV generation are governed by one rule, "What's in it for me?", and are dominated by one maxim, "If it feels good, do it." The quest of the masses is for *joie de vivre* in unbridled and unending excess, the ultimate expression of hedonist society.

In this "enlightened" age of personal freedoms, absolute ethics and demands for standards of conduct are old-hat: they are antiquated relics of the "ignorance" and "superstition" of humankind's best-forgotten past. Religions that have rules for conduct and restraints on immorality are enemies of progress and must be stamped out. The only absolutely absolute that exists for this generation is the understanding that there are absolutely no absolutes. Any restrictions on individual "liberties" must be dealt with in harsh, restrictive ways. The supreme irony is that in a secularized society in which the highest virtue is so-called "tolerance," those who espouse the postmodern ethos are utterly intolerant of those who hold to time-honored, biblically based principles of moral and ethical conduct.

Because of this mentality, everything has been redefined. Even history has been rewritten by revisionists with an agenda of pluralism that includes every position except the absolutist and particularist views of monotheistic faith. Marriage is being redefined, not in biblical terms but in aberrant ones that promote politically correct agendas. Family is being so violently restructured that the "nuclear family" of husband, wife, and children is increasingly threatened with extinction in the postmodern world.

In Europe, neo-paganism and secularism have conspired to overwhelm Christianity, giving rise to a generation that knows not God and lacks even fundamental morality. In Germany, ancient Teutonic gods are openly worshipped with public hedonistic fertility rites that would have made the ancient Greeks and Babylonians blush. France has been described as a perfect example of what a nation can become when it is wholly without God. Britain is but a shell of its former self with the current king-in-waiting expecting his oath of office to include a politically correct commitment to defend all religions, not just the biblical faith to which his ancestors swore fealty.

In much of the former Soviet Union, social experimentation and brainwashing began at tender ages when children were taken from parents and educated by the state so that they became, in effect, state children. In a homogenized society, all homes were the same. They served only as vehicles for the state religion, atheism. This pernicious social experimentation resulted in nations whose malfunctioning moral compasses have so utterly failed that they now find it necessary to invite Western Christians to teach ethics in schools and colleges just to maintain some semblance of civil order.

Likewise, in China, the Chairman-Mao brand of communism has made everyone property of the state and has mandated forced abortions for anyone who dared to threaten the wellbeing of the state by having more than one child. In this process, so many female fetuses have been aborted that mounting numbers of males reaching adulthood find themselves unable to find spouses or to establish families in order to fulfill the most basic instinct of reproduction. This utilitarian view has made the masses in China expendable, including Christians who survive as an underground church only because they decided to believe and practice biblical principles.

Even in nations that were once profoundly clannish and family-centered, the madness of family-bashing has diminished formerly strong family ties. Values that had endured for millennia have been cast to the wind in an all-consuming quest for a homogenized, politically correct world society. Whole nations are being pressured to redefine both marriage and family in categories that are inimical to the health and wellbeing of individuals, children, and society itself—all in the name of equality and tolerance. These societies demand that everything must be tolerated except those religions that require absolutes—Judaism and Christianity. The theorists and bureaucrats of these nations recognize that these enemies of individual "freedom" must eventually be eradicated entirely.

COLD HEART, WARM HEART?

Jesus made the following observation about the age of lawlessness: "Because of the increase of wickedness, the love of most will grow cold."[3] Herein is the root cause of the unrelenting attacks on the institution of the family and home.

Evil triumphs because men of conscience say little and do less. As lawlessness, even hatred of God's laws, becomes more abundant, the love that is the essence of Divine Being diminishes in human hearts and is replaced by an insatiable desire for self-fulfillment and pleasure. The world which once featured much humanitarianism and concern for the downtrodden is ruled by those who think of nothing except self. When men's concerns are only for themselves, there is no depth to which they will not stoop. When men are wrapped up in themselves, they become smaller and smaller packages. They are full of themselves, to be sure, but they have made themselves essentially nothing.

Because of sin, the world has become an increasingly cold and cruel place. The very sanctity of the home has been invaded by these sinister forces, making a growing percentage of homes dark, dreary, and loveless places. Society's heart has been blackened by sin, and love has been crowded out, replaced by self-interest and diverse perversions. Then politicians, bureaucrats, and pundits beat their chest and weep over kids killing kids in schools and on the streets of the metropolises of the West. Then they cite weapons, poverty, and political oppression as the reasons for such violence. As morally bankrupt educators and politicians desperately search for answers to the unthinkable, they blame anything and everything—everything, that is, except the sin that is the real cause of such manifest evil.

Even though iniquity abounds, there is one positive assurance from God's Word: "Where sin increased, grace abounded all the more."[4] God's grace is always superabundant, more than enough to meet every challenge, more than enough to atone for any sin. It is time for the fire of God's loving presence to warm the heart of a cold world. It is time for a renewal movement to sweep over the societies of men throughout the world to bring about a restoration of truly biblical models for home and family. The very existence of civilization is at stake. This is a genuine rallying cry to save the planet. If the insidious postmodernist intentions to destroy the family as it is defined in biblical terms succeeds, civilization as earth has known it will cease to exist, and the world will descend into an abyss of debauchery, violence, and chaos. Without a doubt, it's time for a revolution of restoration. All that is necessary for this manifest evil to succeed is for the righteous of the earth to remain silent in the face of this deliberately planned, carefully orchestrated assault on the biblical family. Now is the time for all good men and women to come to the aid of their planet! Tomorrow may be too late. Everyone must take the position of Hillel the Great: "If I am not for myself, who will be for me, and if I am only for myself, what am I?" and especially Hillel's dictum: "If not now, when?"[5] Indeed, each of those who believe in the biblical family must adopt the motto, "If it's to be, it's up to me."

A CALL FOR RENEWAL

With the profound level of disrespect for authority and the lack of civility and etiquette in large segments of today's society, particularly in the younger generation, a restoration of biblical models for the home is not only a growing need, it is an indispensable requisite for its continued existence. If Western society is to survive the challenges of neo-paganism, monism, and secularism, a "back-to-the-Bible" movement must begin at the most fundamental level of society and the church, the family. New Age philosophy and neo-paganism threaten not only the existence of both Judaism and Christianity but also the very fabric of civilization itself.

Societal renewal begins and continues one family at a time. The nations of the world do not need simply a multi-splendorous manifestation of ecclesiastical triumphalism. And they surely don't need one more massive political or social monstrosity with billions—yea, trillions—of dollars scattered to the wind of political correctness. As a matter of fact, what is needed is not the politically correct but the biblically correct.

Today's societies must be rebuilt from the foundation up. Restoring the family is society's first and foremost need. The world needs millions of Joshuas who will make the resounding proclamation: "As for me and my house, we will serve the LORD."[6] Rather than worrying about the rest of society and seeking to devise strategies to demand societal compliance with biblical morality, leaders are better served by conforming their lives and those of their own families to the mores of God's Word and then witnessing to the decaying world around them by dynamically modeling the success that comes from doing God's thing God's way!

Morality can never be legislated. It is a heart issue. Only changed hearts can conform to the image of God's Son,[7] by "keeping his commandments."[8] Church and societal leaders should do their best to fulfill their public functions, but they must be as King David, who was focused on "blessing his household" even after leading Israel in one of the most ecstatic exercises of worship in recorded history.[9] Church leaders must focus their attention not so much on their ecclesiastical duties as on maintaining a secure domestic temple full of blessing and affirmation for their own families.

To effect change in society and the world, those who are passionate for God's kingdom must begin with society's heart and soul—their own homes. To rebuild battered and ruined cities and nations, each family must restore godliness to itself first. A workable strategy for world renewal and restoration to biblical morality is the one that Nehemiah used to rebuild the ruined city of Jerusalem: every family was directed to work on the part of the wall in front of its house.[10] When believing families restore the biblical home, the inevitable impact will begin to multiply and resound around the globe.

Grace can abound, love can be renewed, and the family can be restored. The biblical ideal can emerge when God's family returns to his guidebook for successful living, the Bible. God can and will create in society a clean heart,[11] but he will do it one family at a time. The coming renewal that will sweep across the world will take place only in the context of the restored family temple.

[1] Baruch HaLevi, and Ellen Frankel, *Revolution of Jewish Spirit: How to Revive Ruakh in Your Spiritual Life, Transform your Synagogue, and Inspire Your Jewish Community* (Woodstock, VT: Jewish Lights Publishing, 2012), p. 67.

[2] Wyatt M. Rogers, Jr. *Christianity and Womanhood* (Westport, Connecticut: Praeger Press, 2002), p. 25.

[3] Matthew 24:12, New International Version.

[4] Romans 5:20, New American Standard Bible (1995).

[5] Hillel, quoted in *Mishnah, Pirkei Avot* 1.14.

[6] Joshua 24:15.

[7] Romans 8:29.

[8] John 14:15.

[9] 2 Samuel 6:20.

[10] Nehemiah 3:23-28

[11] Psalm 51:10.

Chapter 2

Paradise: The Prototype

GOD'S PLAN FOR HEAVEN ON EARTH

The pattern that God used for the creation of the family and the home was first established in heaven itself. In reality, the fundamental social unit for humanity was already in place in the heavenly realm before the earthly creation was summoned into existence by the divine Word.[1] The terrestrial creation was merely a manifestation of the celestial pattern.[2] God's will on earth was first revealed in heaven.[3]

In biblically Hebraic tradition, God is clearly identified as the Heavenly Father, not merely the force of nature that many other religions and philosophies propose. In the "Lord's Prayer," the précis of long-standing Jewish prayer tradition that Jesus taught his disciples, Christians are instructed to address God, not as the Force of Nature or even as the Creator of the universe, but as "our Father."[4] The God of the Bible identifies himself as God in relation to his children. In Jewish tradition, the descriptive title of God becomes crystal clear. He is called *"Avinu, Malkenu"* ("our Father, our King") so that God is addressed first as the father of his children and then as the sovereign of the universe. The God of Scripture is not just the father of humanity's progenitor, Adam, however.[5] He is the God of

Abraham, the God of Isaac, the God of Jacob, and the God and Father of all.[6] Even the angelic hosts of heaven are called his children.[7] He is not, therefore, a static God but an active presence, a God and Father of the living.[8] The very definition of the divine essence, therefore, is that of God, the Father of his children. The core of biblical faith is expressed, not as "May the Force be with you," but as "May the Father be with you."

While the predominant metaphorical image used for God in Scripture is that of father,[9] God is not masculine in gender. As a matter of fact, God is genderless, neither male nor female. Still, God manifests both masculine and feminine qualities and characteristics. This is in keeping with the Hebraic truth that God is not an anthropomorphic creation hatched in the minds of human beings, but that humans are the theomorphic creation of God such that both male and female manifest the divine image in their masculinity and femininity.[10]

Heaven is not, however, an exclusively masculine domain. The Jewish apostle to the nations declared that heavenly Jerusalem is the "mother of us all."[11] The prototype for the earthly Jerusalem (both the literal city and the spiritual city) has a maternal image toward humankind. The angelic hosts of heaven hover in a "motherly manner" over the terrestrial creation. It is a simple biblical truth that every believer, indeed every human being, has a guardian angel who always beholds the Father's face, something that humans are not permitted to do.[12] Angels are given charge over each individual child of God,[13] an assignment that conveys to them a maternal, nurturing relationship. Jewish *aggadot* (traditions) even suggest that each believer has four guardian angels, one in front, one behind, and one on both sides of himself. The corporate heavenly Jerusalem is also the mother of the corporate community of terrestrial believers, the Jerusalem that comes down to earth, a metaphor for the Messiah's bride.[14]

Humankind shares to a lesser degree and dimension[15] the

imbued spark of the divine with which the heavenly creation is infused. When God himself breathed into Adam the breath of life,[16] he deposited in his terrestrial creation a measure of the living Word of God[17] that has caused divine instructions to be impressed upon the heart of every subsequent human being. Paul confirmed this truth by declaring that even those human societies that did not receive God's law (the Torah) still had the fundamentals of that law "written on their hearts.[18] The human conscience is the manifestation of God's character that was God-breathed into humankind and remains a spark of the divine in each human life. The entire human family bears the spiritual image and likeness of its Creator and Father.[19]

God's children, therefore, are part of a heavenly nuclear family, children of a heavenly Father and a heavenly mother. Indeed, in another dimension, God is both father and mother.[20] It should come as no surprise that the heavenly familial pattern was replicated in the earthly family. Heaven came to earth when God formed the first human family in Eden, establishing on planet earth the very first family temple.

The Edenic Ideal

One need look no further than at the record of humanity's creation to understand the value that God placed on the family and the home from time immemorial. After God had completed the creation of the inanimate universe, he turned his focus to the earth, the place where he would deposit life in millions of living organisms. After the myriads of species of plants and animals were in place, God's final creative impulse was to form his crowning creation, the being in whom he would manifest his own image and likeness.[21] He then formed mankind, all of humanity personified in one human being, formed from the dust of the earth but infused with the breath of the Almighty so that he became a living being.

From the moment that God gathered together a handful of dust from the earth and began to shape it, all the genetic coding that would be required for the entire human race was present. The being that God created was called הָאָדָם—*ha-adam* (the adam). This being was the only person in all of Holy Scripture whose name was prefixed in Hebrew by the definite article ה—*ha* ("the").[22] This was not *Adam*, a solitary male being, but *ha-adam*, "the adam," or the human. In reality, the Hebrew term *ha-adam* simply described the very essence of all humanity: "The Earth Being." The word *adam* is derived from the word *adamah*, which means "ground," "humus" or "dirt." The play on words is obvious: *ha-adam* was formed from *ha-adamah*, the human from the humus, the earthling from the earth.

After God had assembled the correct proportions of terrestrial dust, he structured the first being of humanity and vivified that lifeless form with his divine breath, the breath of life. More than the *nefesh* ("life") that he shared with all the animal creation, *ha-adam* was a *living* being, infused with the divine breath of life (*neshamah*). In reality, Scripture confirms that God breathed into *ha-adam* "the breaths of lives" (נִשְׁמַת חַיִּים)—*nishmat hayim*[23] so that both male and female and all their subsequent progeny were somehow present in *ha-adam* from the moment that God created the first human being. *Ha-adam* was, indeed, the corporate head of all humanity.

At the very moment of this being's formation, the adam was both male and female. "God created man in his own image . . . male and female created he *them*."[24] A subsequent biblical summary of this divine creative moment makes this declaration: "Male and female created he them; and blessed them, and called *their* name [שְׁמָם] Adam [אָדָם], in the day that *they* were created."[25] From the moment of humanity's creation, the name given to the human entity, both male and female, was *Adam*. They, both male and female, were called "Adam." The newly formed being was not the genderless androgyne of mythology, nor was it a hermaphrodite. It was also not simply a male creation. It was humanity. All the genetic material necessary for gender-specific existence was present in the human body from the moment God formed it from the dust of the earth.

FOUNDATION OF FAMILY

The formation of "woman" was not a divine afterthought when the omniscient God suddenly came to realize that his new male creation lacked companionship. Nor was woman's creation God's effort to rectify a divine mistake by forming a secondary and inferior servant gender by constructing her from masculine spare parts. The formation of Eve represented the separation from the adam of that part of humanity that was feminine and the formation of a body-and-spirit entity that was complementary in every way to the masculine remnant of original humanity. The only difference between the two beings that existed after the divine surgery was their gender: Adam was אִישׁ (*ish*), male; Eve was אִשָּׁה (*ishshah*), female. Both were still *ha-adam*, humanity, and both were still called by God, "Adam." This was the Edenic foundation of family.

After he anesthetized *ha-adam*, God removed from the earth being an anatomical part that has for centuries been defined as a "rib." The word in Hebrew is צֶלַע (*tzela*), which elsewhere in Scripture is translated "side,"[26] "chamber,"[27] "beam,"[28] "brow (of a hill),"[29] or "to limp, stumble, or be lame."[30] The only place in Scripture where the word *tzela* is translated "rib" is in the human creation narrative.

The translation of the Hebrew word *tzela* as "rib" became possible because of the association of the word *side* with the skeletal structure that supports the sides of a human body, the rib cage. Before the second century BC, however, there is no evidence for the translation of *tzela* as "rib." Indeed, πλευρά (*pluera*), the Greek word that translates *tzela* from Hebrew, was also consistently used to mean "side" in classical Greek until the same time. Perhaps because of the association of *tzela* with the arched beams of the temple or with the brow (rib) of a hill, it came to be translated "rib." Indeed, since the beginning of the Common Era, *tzela* has been the Hebrew word for "rib."

If, indeed, the woman were constructed from a "rib" of the man, Adam either had an extra rib before the surgery or afterwards had a deficiency that was not transmitted to subsequent male progeny. On the other hand, *tzela* could speak figuratively or could even be translated "chamber" as a euphemism for uterus ("arched side chamber") and related organs that would have been a logical basis for the formation of the first female being. Whatever the case, all the genetic material necessary for the construction of woman was present in the side of "the adam" from the moment of human creation. Indeed, the removal of that material left a void which God "closed up with flesh."[31]

From this statement, many theologians over the centuries have even suggested (with amazing anatomical inaccuracy!) that men have one less rib than women,[32] and others have extrapolated the preposterous idea that "feminine guile" is the result of woman's creation from a "crooked bone."[33] This idea has reinforced the perception that femininity is inferior to masculinity, as though the male Adam had a superfluous anatomical part that God used to create an assistant to the superior male creation. It has also helped perpetuate the insidious idea that women are inherently evil, masters of feminine guile by which they seduce and corrupt men.[34]

The narrative of Eve's formation is interesting in that it declares that "God made an *ishshah* [woman] from the *tzela* [side or side chamber] he had taken out of [or away from] *ha-Adam* [humankind]."[35] When God brought the woman to Adam, the man exclaimed, "At last, this one is now bone of my bone and flesh of my flesh," and he called her, "*ishshah* [woman], because she was taken out of *ish* [man]."[36] The divine narrative declares that the woman was taken from humankind (*ha-adam*), while the remaining masculine being recognized his new companion as having been taken from man (*ish*), or from himself.

Even though the Hebrew word *ishshah* is not etymologically connected with the word *ish*, the author of the Genesis narrative employed a play on words by comparing the assonance of the Hebrew words *ish* (man) and *ishshah* (woman) to have the man say, "She shall be called woman (*ishshah*) because she was taken from man (*ish*)." The now-masculine Adam realized right away that what was standing before him was genuinely a part of himself, not another species, not some other substance or inferior creation, but a being equally human who was complementary to himself in every way. She was to him, "bone of my bone and flesh of my flesh."

Before God separated Eve from *ha-adam*, he had brought before the human entity all the animal creation so that Adam could name each of them. It then became clear to God's human creation that none of these beings was comparable to mankind. God also observed that it was "not good" for the human to live alone as a solitary being. Whereas before that time, God's entire creation had been "good," now for the first time, something was lacking: the absence of suitable companionship for God's crowning creation had become "not good." The "good" creation had not suddenly become "bad": it was simply not good enough.

God, therefore, separated the feminine gender of humankind from the masculine gender. The result was one man (*ish*) and one woman and (*ishshah*)—two separate, yet equal beings with complementary genders. This is why, when Adam first saw Eve, he exclaimed, "At last!" After viewing and naming all the other animal creations, he could without hesitation recognize that this creature was from, of, and for himself. It was like seeing the essence of his own being flashed before him in a mirror, all personified in Eve! Here was his true alter-ego.

The separation of the *tzela* and the subsequent formation of Eve in no way weakened Adam. The fact that woman was formed around something that was described as an "arched chamber" similar to those side chambers in Solomon's temple should suggest that the woman brought a unique strength to the new human family. Just as the arch is one of the strongest of all architectural structures, so woman has always had an inner strength that has brought a life-saving help to man and has strengthened him for the role that God has designed for him.

Just as God had not been content to dwell in isolation but had created the hosts of heaven, so it was not good for *ha-adam* to remain alone. Humanity was designed by God to be a gregarious creation. The reclusive ascetic is the exception to the rule. Withdrawal from social interaction is aberrant behavior, contrary to the divine intent and the divine instruction. Even celibacy is not the biblical norm.[37] God's very first commandment to human beings was to "be fruitful and multiply and fill the earth,"[38] and that commandment has never been abrogated. All human beings, therefore, fully realize their humanity and their God-given potential in the context of marriage and family.

COMPLEMENTARY COMPANIONSHIP

The sole purpose for the separation of humanity into two genders, then, was for the creation of interpersonal relationship, a sublime fellowship of counterbalancing mutual affirmation. This was the cure for the aloneness and isolation that was "not good" for humanity. From the beginning of human generation, therefore, God's design was for the companionship and communion of complementary beings. Indeed, when both male and female were rejoined by God as husband and wife, for the very first time, the creation was called "very good."[39]

The basis for the common unity of the human community was established in God's stated intention for separating Eve from Adam. The surgery was not designed to create division and conflict: it was for the purpose of producing a multifaceted unity. When God observed that it was not good for humanity to be alone, he purposed to create an "equal partner" for him.[40] The Hebrew term עֵזֶר כְּנֶגְדּוֹ (*ezer kenegdo*), meaning "equal partner," was translated "help meet" ("qualified helper") in the sixteenth-century King James Version of the Bible. The term *help meet* later morphed into the neologism *helpmate*. The inadequate understanding of the Hebrew term *ezer kenegdo* allowed various church traditions to adduce "scriptural" evidence to support their insistence on the inferiority and subordination of women to men.

In Hebrew, however, *ezer kenegdo* in no way implies inferiority. *Ezer* is the same word which is used to describe God as man's "help." "The LORD . . . is our help [*ezer*] and our shield,"[41] said the Psalmist. Certainly there is no thought of inferiority in God because he is the helper (*ezer*) of humankind! Why, then, should inferiority be assumed and ascribed to woman as man's *ezer*? In reality, the context of the feminine formation narrative implies the truth. God purposed to create a power comparable to or equal to Adam and in order to do so, he separated a part of *ha-adam* and around it fashioned (literally, "built up") Eve. The woman was neither inferior to nor superior to the man. She was his complement, his equal. She was his help and shield, a means of security and solidarity.

Eve was Adam's perfect counterbalance who brought inner strength, wisdom, and insight to their joint life. Because she was made of something from inside Adam, she was gifted with intuition, the ability to see through façades into the innermost motives and to discern with visceral feeling, not rationalization or analysis.[42] In order for Adam to have these insights, he needed a "help," his wife. Likewise, Eve lacked a part of what was left in Adam and consequently had an innate "inclination" toward her husband[43] to resort to the elements of strength, drive, and provision that he brings to the superentity of the two-in-one. Theirs was to be more than a partnership, it was to be an equal covenantal relationship in which both counterbalanced and complemented the other in a manner that mirrored the love of the Creator himself.

This truth is further established in the second part of the appellative for woman, *ezer kenegdo*. It contains two prepositions, *k-* (כ) and *neged* (נֶגֶד) before the pronoun *o* (וֹ). *K-* means "like." *Neged* means "over against" or "in front of." *O* means "him." The prepositional phrase *kenegdo*, then, means "like," but "over against" or "in front of" him. It can also mean "in opposition to"; however, it is clear from the context that it implies a qualified counterbalance that was to bring a measure of strength to the human interpersonal relationship that the man could not offer. The implication in the "help-meet" passage is that Eve is "equal to or adequate to" Adam. Eve was to be a counterbalance to Adam, elevating the quality of their relationship and reinforcing their unity by adding what her husband lacked.

The use of the word *neged* to mean "in front of" also implies the unique relationship that Adam and Eve and their subsequent counterparts of masculine and feminine humanity would enjoy above all others. They were to have a "face-to-face" relationship of mutual respect and affirmation toward one another, a relationship akin to the *panim el-panim* (face-to-face) intimacy that Adam and Eve also had with God in the garden.[44] From Eden onward, the foundation of the human family would be the open and unashamed relationship between one man and one woman. The woman was not to be in a subservient position several paces behind the man. She was to be in front of him, facing him, exchanging mutually affirming love with him. She was to be *kenegdo*: "like" (*k-*) while at the same time being "over against" (*-neged-*) him (*-o*). They were to be on the same level as equal beings who, by divine design, possessed different physical and emotional characteristics that complemented and counter-balanced each other.

Even the physical intimacy experienced in the human family was a manifestation of the one-to-one, face-to-face relationship of equality and openness. When Adam and Eve fulfilled God's first commandment to "be fruitful and multiply," they became "one flesh." What God had merged into one through the covenant of marriage was now intertwined in loving conjugation. Unlike the rest of the animal creation, the human couple shared their intimacy in a face-to-face, mouth-to-mouth embrace. Their anatomy was so designed that especially in their most intimate and passionate moment, they were *panim el-panim*, complementary equals facing and embracing each other.

The manifestation of the female was also for the purpose of completing the male, not for canceling or opposing him. Femininity is a counterbalance to masculinity and vice versa. When humankind became two, both halves were necessary for optimum efficiency in the human family. Without the woman, man would be eccentric, out of balance. Likewise, without the man, the woman would be discordant, lacking equanimity. Men and women were simply never designed by God to be identical. They have always possessed different, yet complementary characteristics. They fulfill different, yet mutually reciprocal roles. For this reason alone, modern society's insistence upon a politically correct "unisex" view of men and women is an affront to both God and nature. Indeed, if male and female were identical, one of the two would be superfluous. God would never have made two if one were adequate to complete his purposes.

It is for this reason that Judaism has long taught that every human being has another half. It is foundational not only to the ongoing survival of the human species but also to the health of the human family that men and women find and be reconnected with their other half. From a purely Hebraic standpoint, therefore, celibacy is not an option for either men or women. It is God's design that the two be made one as was demonstrated in the Edenic ideal. Two males or two females cannot be complete together, for both male and female are required to form the superentity of oneness that is complete. While male and female in and of themselves are complete personalities, it is marriage that brings together these complete persons into a new and unique completeness in the ultimate mutually fulfilling interpersonal relationship. What the husband lacks, the wife adds. What the wife needs, the husband provides. By divine design, they perfectly complement each other, making the whole of marriage greater than the sum of its parts.

TWO BEINGS, ONE FAMILY

The restoration of the original oneness of humanity by bringing together a man and a woman was not solely for the perpetuation of the human species. The fact that man and woman can be joined anatomically into oneness is a by-product of the oneness that God designed for the human family. Oneness is first a spiritual unity achieved through divinely commissioned agreement called "covenant." The covenant of marriage is unique in that it involves three persons—man, woman, and

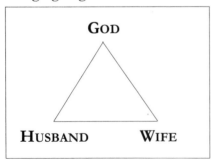

The strongest geometric structure is a triangle. Likewise, the family is at its strongest when husband and wife are totally committed and mutually submitted laterally to each another in covenant equality, and both are vertically submitted to God.

God—and in that it was designed from the beginning to be indissoluble.[45] This kind of relationship creates the strongest of geometric structures, with God at the top of the triangle and man and woman on an equal plane at the bottom. Some Jewish scholars have suggested that even in marital conjugation, three persons are involved: husband, wife, and God.[46] This is why the Jewish concept of marriage is that of merger, not just a partnership.[47]

The unity that creates a family is not uniformity, a unisex state of sameness where the blurring of identities and roles dominates and confuses. It is a state of pluriformity, a unity in diversity that is manifest in cohesion. This is the biblical definition of unity. It is the state of being *echad* (one), a oneness similar in nature (though not in degree) to the oneness of God himself, who is also declared to be *echad* in the most fundamental statement of Jewish and Christian faith, the *Shema*: "Hear, O Israel, the LORD our God is one [*echad*] LORD."[48]

The reunification of man and woman, then, was the essence of God's first instruction to humanity immediately after Eve was separated from Adam. "Hence a man leaves his father and mother and clings to his wife, so that they become one flesh."[49] The King James Version's translation of this passage is more memorable than most others, for it says that a man is to "leave" and "cleave"—leave his parents and cleave to his wife so that they subsequently become "one flesh." It is interesting that God said that a man should leave his parents and be joined to his wife, not that the woman should leave her parents and be joined to her husband. While most cultures, including Christian ones, have required the woman to leave her family and be joined to her husband, God says just the opposite!

From the formation of the very first family in Eden, it has been clear that the social order for the human creation would be this: man and woman would leave their paternal and maternal relationships to form a new entity replicating that first social unit—one man and one woman joined together in an *echad* of ultimate unity. The sexual consummation of the marriage merely demonstrates physically what has already been accomplished spiritually by divine covenant. Two have become one, merged into a mystical oneness that only God can fully understand. Indeed, their "oneness" has become so absolute that their "twoness" has ceased to exist, just as Jesus himself explicitly and unequivocally declared: "They are no longer two, but one flesh."[50]

Marriage was designed to be the cement that joins together the fundamental societal unit in an ever-strengthening bond. Indeed, what God has joined together, man is not to put asunder.[51] Husband and wife were to be "glued together," as the Hebrew word דָּבַק (*dabak*), which is generally translated "join" or "cleave" is more accurately rendered.[52] Skip Moen has vividly and memorably called this *dabak* "super glue."[53] Marriage was not to be a casual, intermittent relationship based solely on emotional or hormonal responses. It was to be a life-long covenantal relationship that would provide a secure, stable environment for the nurturing of children and the perpetuation of the human family. Malachi established this as the fundamental reason for God's making husband and wife one: "Did not [God] make them one? And why one? Because he seeks godly offspring."[54] Marriage then truly represents a divine bonding that creates a unity, a superentity that is greater than its constituent parts.

Not only did Adam and Eve fit together anatomically, they were suited to each another in every way. They fit together emotionally, intellectually, spiritually. Everything that one needed was found in the other. They were the full realization of total humanity in male and female that had been returned to unity. They complemented each another. They were perfect counterparts. They provided each other with counterbalanced mutuality. As they were cemented in indissoluble unity, neither had any lack.

Their oneness was the perfect state for adding to the human family the children that God purposed for them. Though sin entered in and brought dysfunctionality to the family of humanity, God's intention was clear. The human family was patterned after the heavenly design. God's tabernacle was with humanity. He had created a family temple.

The human family, therefore, has always been and will always be defined by its most fundamental unit, the nuclear family. What God originally instituted in Eden was to be the pattern for all subsequent ideal manifestations of humanity. The institution of the family was to be the basis for the social interaction of all humankind. Only when the sanctity of the home is upheld, therefore, is a foundation established for security and growth both in the church and in society.

HEAVEN ON EARTH

The quality of the divine relationship between the heavenly Father and the heavenly Jerusalem was the pattern for the Edenic family. The original center for social and spiritual development was the garden home. Loving, affirming relationships made that home a true sanctuary. There was no physical temple, no tabernacle, not even a chapel. Every social interaction and every act of worship was carried out solely in the context of the family. The home was the true temple.

Since the time when God created the first family, that pattern has been replicated generation after generation as humans leave, cleave, and multiply, fulfilling the divine plan for maintaining the image of God on planet earth. Heaven continues to be manifest on earth in the form of the home. The ideal family is a paradise in itself, a true sanctuary of safety and repose. God's heavenly pattern always works when properly employed on earth.

Interestingly enough, the sages of Israel have long viewed God as a matchmaker, insisting that the work in which he has engaged himself since he completed the Genesis creation has been the making of marriages and families. It is God's purpose to bring together the separated halves of the human family, the man and woman who are intended for each other. If this is true, marriage is really the proverbial "match made in heaven."

The human longing for companionship and the fulfillment of the divine command for marital union has been innate in the psyche and in the hormonal chemistry—even the DNA—of human existence. God uses what he has formed naturally in humanity to fulfill his purposes in replicating the original family in their garden home, the ever-renewed paradise that God created for humankind, the family temple.

[1] Colossians 1:16; John 1:3.

[2] Hebrews 8:5.

[3] Matthew 6:10.

[4] Matthew 6:9.

[5] Luke 3:37.

[6] Luke 20:37-38.

[7] Job 1:6; 38:7.

[8] Exodus 4:4. In defining himself as the God of Abraham, the God of Isaac, and the God of Jacob, the Eternal manifest himself as a God of the living, not of the long-dead (Matthew 22:32). He was not just Adam's Father; he is the Father of all (Ephesians 4:6).

[9] There are various metaphorical images in Scripture that represent God as having a feminine and maternal nature (e.g., the God who is the Creator/Father in Exodus 3:6 is the God who gave birth to Israel as noted in Isaiah 49:15). In reality, however, God is genderless Spirit, and the anthropomorphisms that Scripture ascribes to him are material means of communicating understanding about God. Romans 1:20 declares that the invisible God is understood (but never worshipped) through the things that are made.

[10] Genesis 1:26-27.

[11] Galatians 4:26.

[12] Matthew 18:10; 1 Timothy 6:16.

[13] Psalm 91:11.

[14] Revelation 21:2, 9-10.

[15] Psalm 8:5; Hebrews 2:7, 9.

[16] Genesis 2:7

[17] 2 Timothy 3:16. The Holy Scriptures are the God-breathed manifestation of the living Word, the divine *Logos* (John 1:1-4).

[18] Romans 2:15. Man's conscience is a spark of divinity, the imprint of the divine in the form of the foundational commandments for human conduct that are written on all men's hearts.

[19] Genesis 9:6. In this passage, God told Noah that anyone who commits murder must be punished by death because every human being is made in the image of God.

[20] God chose to image himself as both father and mother in the pages of Holy Scripture. This is very clear from Deuteronomy 32:18. In the summary of God's dealings with Israel at the close of Moses' career, God himself spoke of his relationship with Israel in this way: "Of the Rock who created (יְלָדְךָ—*yeladcha*) you, you were unmindful, and you have forgotten the God who writhed in labor with you (הַמְחֹלְלֶךָ—*cholelecha*)." This second part of this passage has been mistranslated in order to obscure the "mothering" image of God with renderings like, "You have forgotten the God who *fathered* you" (NKJV, emphasis added). It is a simple biological fact, however, that men do not "writhe in labor" when they "father" a child. God, therefore, specifically declared to Israel that they were not mindful of the God who "fathered" them and had forgotten the God who "mothered" them.

[21] Genesis 1:26

[22] Scripture never calls Abraham *ha-Avraham* (the-Abraham) or David *ha-David* (the-David). Adam is called *ha-adam* because this being was not just a human male, but all of humanity.

[23] Genesis 2:7.

[24] Genesis 1:27, emphasis added.

[25] Genesis 5:2, emphasis added.

[26] Exodus 25:12; 26:35; 30:4; Job 18:11; 1 Kings 6:8.

[27] 1 Kings 6:5, 8; Ezekiel 41:5, 9-11, 26.

[28] 1 Kings 6:15.

[29] 2 Samuel 13:34.

[30] Psalm 35:15; 38:17; Micah 4:7; Zephaniah 3:19. *Tzela* is translated "lame" in most versions.

[31] Genesis 2:21, New International Version.

[32] When sixteenth-century scientist Vesalius, the father of studies in human anatomy, proved that men and women both have 24 ribs, he was roundly assailed as a heretic because the church and most of society believed that all men had one less rib than all women because Adam had a "rib" surgically removed. See Howard W. Haggard, *From Medicine Man to Doctor: The Story of the Science of Healing* (New York: Harper and Brothers Publishers, 1929), p. 111.

[33] Hugh W. Sanborn, ed., *Celebrating Passages in the Church: Reflections and Resources* (St. Louis, MO: Chalice Press, 1999), p. 17.

[34] Heinrich Kramer and James Sprenger, *The Malleus Maleficarum of Heinrich Kramer and James Sprenger*, tr. Montague Summers (Mineola, NY: Dover Publications, 1971), p. 44. *Malleus Maleficarum* literally meant "the hammer of malefactresses [witches]." Kramer and Sprenger argued that "there was a defect in the formation of the first woman, since she was formed from a bent rib, that is, a rib of the breast, which is bent as it were in a contrary direction to man. And since through this defect she is an imperfect animal, she always deceives." This argument was used to legitimize the torture and murder of women who were judged to be witches during the Inquisition.

[35] Genesis 2:22, New International Version.

[36] Genesis 2:23, New International Version.

[37] Celibacy has been preferred in times of great persecution (1 Corinthians 7:27) and by those who have made the sacrifice of depriving themselves of companionship in order to advance the kingdom of God (Matthew 19:12). This, however, is a personal choice and never a divine requirement. God's commandment is that human beings should marry and create a family: "Leave father and mother and be joined together . . . be fruitful and multiply and fill the earth." Rabbinic Judaism has insisted that any person who is not married is incomplete and is in violation of the divine commandment to "be fruitful and multiply." In Jewish history, however, there is evidence of sages who were bachelors (at least until later

life). Jesus himself was not married even at the age of 33. Additionally, those who were widowed at an early age often never remarried (cf. Luke 2:36-37, where Anna, the prophetess, who had been widowed only seven years after her wedding, subsequently lived much of her remaining years in the temple complex and was 84 at the time of Jesus' birth). For detailed analysis of this and other mistranslations of Scripture that have been designed to reinforce the masculine image of God while minimizing the feminine images of God, see John D. Garr, *God and Women: Woman in God's Image and Likeness* (Atlanta, GA: Golden Key Press, 2011), pp. 109-147, especially pp.113-119.

[38] Genesis 1:28.

[39] Genesis 1:22.

[40] Genesis 2:18.

[41] Psalm 33:20; cf. 115:11, King James Version; cf. Psalm 70:5; 124:8; Hosea 3:9.

[42] Muriel Mohabir, "A Woman Designed by God," in *Sisters with Power,* Joe Eldred, ed. (London: Cortemus, 2000), p. 125.

[43] God's description to the woman of the consequences of the human couple's sin has been translated as "Your desire shall be to your husband, and he shall rule over you" (Genesis 3:16). The Hebrew word translated almost universally as "desire" (sometimes "sexual desire") is תְּשׁוּקָתֵֿהֶם (*teshuqah*), which literally means "turning," implying "inclination."

[44] *Panim el-panim* (פָּנִים אֶל־פָּנִים) is the ideal state of intimacy with God that the righteous achieved in Scripture (cf. Moses in Exodus 33:11).

[45] Though divorce was acceptable in Hebraic culture under given sets of circumstances, Jesus made it clear that God's original intent was for marital permanence (cf. Matthew 19:6-8). In verse 9 of this passage Jesus also established the principal legitimate reason for divorce and remarriage as marital infidelity. Paul further approved divorce and remarriage for abandonment, indicating that failure to fulfill the contract of the marriage covenant can result in its being voided (cf. 1 Corinthians 7:15).

[46] Nachmanides, *Iggeret ha-Kodesh [The Holy Epistle].* Nachmanides says, "When a man unites with his wife in holiness, the *Shekinah* is between them in the mystery of man and woman."

[47] Robert O. Samms, *Making Marriage Meaningful: Insights and Secrets from a Forty Year Marriage* (Lincoln, NE: iUniverse, 2005), p. 218.

[48] Deuteronomy 6:4. This declaration of the *Shema* is the rock-solid foundation of Jewish faith; however, it is also the first and greatest commandment of Christian faith. Jesus himself said, when asked which was the first and greatest commandment, "The foremost is, Hear, O Israel! The LORD our God is one LORD" (Mark 12:29, NASB).

[49] Matthew 19:5.

[50] Matthew 19:6a.

[51] Matthew 19:6b.

[52] Genesis 2:24, Jewish Publication Society *Tanakh.*

[53] Skip Moen, *Guardian Angel: What You Must Know about God's Design for Women* (Charleston, SC: Blue Sky Ministries, 2011), p. 121.

[54] Malachi 2:15, NIV.

Chapter 3

The Domestic Temple

CENTER FOR HUMAN DEVELOPMENT

Adam and Eve communed with God when the Creator came to their garden home in the cool of the day.[1] They did not go to a shrine that God had built for them. God came to them in their home—the very first house church! Their home was a natural place for worship and communion. It was a domestic temple. It needed no embellishment or grandiose, imposing façade. Everything was simple. It was just Adam and Eve—the first family—and God. The progenitors of the human race walked with God in a sweet communion of blissful joy and fulfillment.

Even after Adam and Eve sinned by violating God's commandment, the human family was not given a physical temple in which to repose in order to commune with him. Indeed, the process continued as the simple act of "walking with God."[2] For those descendants of Adam who remained faithful to God, the Eternal was an ever-present reality, not some distant, inaccessible being or one who could be approached only in the confines of a specific space. The prototype in heaven was replicated in the human family on earth. The heavenly temple, as it were, came down to man and was manifest in the home.

Enoch, the seventh from Adam, was so dedicated to this

divine walk with God that he was translated from earth to God's presence and never experienced death.[3] Subsequently the divine order for family disintegrated when the sons of God married the daughters of men.[4] Finally, only Noah had maintained the purity of his genealogy.[5] As a result he "found grace in the eyes of the LORD"[6] and saved humanity from the universal flood by constructing the ark, which became his own family sanctuary. Salvation from the deluge was accomplished in the context of family. The family, therefore, was the locus for spiritual relationship in the beginning of time, and it continued to be the focal point of life throughout the patriarchal age.

A TENT: ABRAHAM AND SARAH'S FAMILY TEMPLE

Sarah and Abraham's tent was a shining example of the family temple. Though theirs was a transient, nomadic existence, still they had a fixed and continuing temple, their family home. Their tent was their place of fellowship, study, and prayer. Though Abraham appeared before the king-priest of Salem to make an offering and receive a blessing,[7] his principal venue for interaction with God was his own home, with his own family and the myriads of guests who frequented his portable temple.

Rabbinic tradition asserts that Sarah's tent was open on all four sides, demonstrating the profound hospitality of her home.[8] It also suggests that Sarah was such a powerful prophetess that she is believed to be the first woman to whom the powerful ode of praise to the Woman of Valor was sung as a eulogy.[9] Sarah and Abraham's tent-temple was so holy that God, accompanied by two angels, did not hesitate to walk in, sit down, share table fellowship with them and make inviolable, unimpeachable promises to both Abraham and Sarah—the first family of faith.[10]

Abraham became the father of the faithful because he believed God so much that he did not hesitate to carry out God's instructions.[11] He also ensured the fact that his descendants after him would do justice and love mercy by instructing them as they worshipped together in their family temple.[12] Abraham's faithfulness in family worship and teaching was the principal reason that God gave for selecting him as the progenitor of the faith race.

Until the time when God brought the Hebrew descendants of Abraham to Sinai and there constituted them as the nation of Israel, all the worship functions of the Abrahamic family were carried out in the context of their home. Even the great event that brought the Israelites freedom from Egyptian slavery was manifest not in corporate worship in an imposing temple but in family worship in each humble Israelite home. "Place the lamb's blood on the doorposts and lintels of your houses," the children of Israel were instructed, "and remain in your houses, eating the roasted lamb and the bread of haste (*matzah*)."[13] Surely God could have had Moses instruct Aaron to sacrifice one lamb for all of Israel in a solemn public ceremony filled with pomp and circumstance. Would not one great liturgical exercise for all would have been far more economical and have made more sense? But, the action that brought salvation to Israel was a family affair. Moses had instructed the Israelites: "Each man is to take a lamb for his family, one for each household."[14] God was determined to deliver all of Israel; however, his plan for their deliverance was executed one family at a time through worship that lasted the entire night in each Israelite family temple!

From the time of the Exodus until the present day, the primary annual worship experience for the descendants of those who were delivered from Egypt has been the Passover. The divine appointment has been celebrated from year to year for millennia in the context of each Jewish family as it was on that first Passover night. Parents and grandparents lead their families in this act of remembrance which God enjoined that night upon the Israelites throughout all their generations, forever.[15] All family members, from the oldest to the youngest, celebrate the fact that they were personally delivered from Egypt.[16]

For the Jewish people even today, the entire Passover celebration remains first and foremost a family worship experience. In the spirit of the hospitality that is so essential to the Jewish mindset, the family temple is also expanded to include extended family members (aunts, uncles, cousins, nephews, and nieces), friends, and even strangers. The family temple is not designed to be a closed, exclusive circle limited to an elite few. It is to be an open, inclusive company that welcomes others to share in the sanctity of family worship and fellowship.

Following the Exodus, the Hebrew family became God's nation, a kingdom of priests.[17] Assembled at Sinai, all the families of the Israelites were organized into one extended family, the corporate assembly of Israel. The newly birthed nation received a constitution, the Torah, which was an outline of God's instructions to his children. Within that constitution were instructions of how the unified family of Israel as a corporate entity should worship in covenant relationship with God. In effect, the thousands of home churches in the Sinai desert became history's largest megachurch, one of perhaps two million people!

When the worshipping community met for fellowship, study, and worship, it was described biblically as a "congregation."[18] Congregations can be of any size that is practical; however, as Moses' father-in-law Jethro advised him, his two million member congregation was too large and needed to be subdivided into communities of one hundred, fifty, and ten.[19] Still, the fundamental unit of every corporate body has always been and must always be the family. The fundamental temple is the family temple.

GOD'S TENT—MAN'S TENT

In order to facilitate corporate worship and to systematize and standardize a uniform order for personal and family devotion, God instructed Moses to build a sanctuary, a *mishkan* (tabernacle).

This structure was to be portable, and it was to be housed in a tent. God's sanctuary was to go with the people, not vice versa.[20] The central elements of that material structure were transportable, designed in such a way that they could be dismantled when necessary so that they could accompany the Israelites wherever God led them. God's house had no fixed dwelling place. It was simply with his people. Just as God had maintained personal contact with the foundational entity of his society, the home, so the tabernacle in the wilderness was established to function in the midst of the camp of Israel: God's tent was right in the middle of all the family tents of this transient people.

The implements and appliances of God's house were not mystifying objects that were beyond the comprehension of all but a monastic, priestly class. They were objects that reflected ordinary Hebrew family values. The laver that demanded ritual purity of the priests and the sacrifices was but a formal manifestation of the Israelites' concern with personal cleanliness. "Change your garments and be clean," their father Jacob had already commanded them after his encounter with God at Peniel.[21] The table of the bread of the divine presence merely underscored their understanding that God was the one who brought forth bread from the earth and rained down bread from heaven for their sustenance in the desert.[22] Indeed, the continuing Jewish use of two loaves of *challah* bread in the *Shabbat* celebration is a memorial

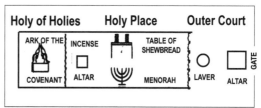

This diagram shows the three distinct divisions of Israel's wilderness sanctuary which replicated the three sections of Abraham's tent home. Every home, like the ancient synagogue should be a House of Meeting (Outer Court, the place of meeting), a House of Study (the Holy Place with its symbols of the Word of God, the shewbread and the menorah), and a House of Prayer (Holy of Holies, the place of worship.)

of the bread of the presence that was arranged in two rows on the table. The menorah was a manifestation of the light that had symbolized the divine presence in their homes long before it did so in the sanctuary. The altar of incense was a reflection of the Israelites' love of spices and the aromas of sweetness that contrasted with the malodorous smell of life among the various animals that were essential to their nomadic existence. The portable sanctuary, therefore, was patterned after the Israelite tent home, dating back to Sarah and Abraham's tent and beyond.

After Israel inherited the Promised Land, the focus of worship remained with the family. The primary vehicle for social and worship activities continued to be the home. No greater illustration of this truth can be found than in the narrative of one of Israel's most exhilarating corporate worship experiences. When King David returned the Ark of the Covenant to prominence in Israel, he led the assembled multitude in ecstatic praise, dancing before the Lord with all his might.[23] What a profound public demonstration of passionate devotion to the God of Israel! David's thoughts, however, were not lost in this profound exercise of the momentary existential experience of public worship. When he had completed the public function of his office, he immediately retired to his own home for this express purpose: "David returned to bless his household."[24]

Even though there were priests in Israel who had been specifically commissioned with the responsibility of bestowing God's blessing on the children of Israel,[25] David remembered his primary role as the leader of his household and returned from a great corporate worship exercise to his family temple so he, as the priest of his home, could bless his family. David's home, not the congregation or its establishment for religion, was his primary sanctuary of blessing and the place for his personal devotion.

At a later time, David wanted to replicate or even exceed

the splendor of his own palace in a national temple for all Israel.[26] He purposed to build God a house. Interestingly enough, God did not command David to build this structure as he had instructed Moses to build the tabernacle. He did, however, allow Solomon to complete the task. The magnificent temple was completed by Solomon on the same site where Abraham had offered Isaac centuries before. At that time, the official religion of Israel was established for the first time in a fixed location, in the Jerusalem temple.

THE HOME AS A TEMPLE IN MINIATURE

After many generations, the political leadership and the temple cultus became so corrupt and oppressive that God himself summoned a pagan king to destroy both. Nebuchadnezzar, the Babylonian king, overwhelmed Jerusalem, destroyed the palaces and the temple, and led the people away in chains of captivity. Faced with the loss of the very implements and system of worship that they had come to trust, the Israelites were challenged to find an alternate means of worshipping God. By the rivers of Babylon, they hung their harps on the willows and lamented, "How can we sing the LORD's songs in a foreign land?"[27]

Their grief over the loss of their corporate sanctuary, however, could not suppress their passion for worshipping God. After a time, they recognized that God could again be worshipped in the context of their own homes and in smaller corporate exercises in the same way in which he had been honored before both the tabernacle and the temple had been built. They came to realize that the center of worship had always been the home and that the corporate exercises of worship to which they had been called[28] could be fulfilled apart from the temple cultus. What eventually became formalized in their understanding and belief was first a practical reality in their lives. Their homes once again became mini-temples. Then, as families assembled for fellowship, study, and corporate worship, their meetings also became mini-temple experiences.

In the exile, the emphasis of worship was returned to the people, to the family, and to the extended family or corporate community, which eventually became known as the synagogue. There was no temple and no other formal structures that were dedicated exclusively to worship. Indeed, in that time, there were no buildings called synagogues. The synagogues were meetings (reunions), and those synagogues assembled in homes or in public places. The family was the church, and the church was the extended family, the congregation.[29] Buildings were not the object of worship: God was! And God could be worshipped in the most humble of sanctuaries, even in the hovel of a slave family's hut.

When Israel returned from captivity to rebuild Jerusalem and the temple, the newly discovered (perhaps even newly restored) institution of the synagogue continued. Worship could be maintained even without a central geographical focus. It could be manifest in each meeting of the people, whether that meeting was merely a single family assembled for study and devotion or hundreds or even thousands of members of a community assembled as a congregation.

By the time of Jesus, the synagogue was a firmly established institution in Israel and beyond. As a matter of fact, there were nearly 500 synagogues in Jerusalem at the time when the earliest Christian movement was birthed from the matrix of biblical and second-temple Judaism.[30] Across the Mediterranean basin and beyond, wherever the Jewish people journeyed, they took with them the tradition of the synagogue and established new meetings for the purpose of fellowship, study, and worship.

The earliest church simply continued this tradition. As long as the disciples of Jesus were welcome in the synagogues, they were faithful to join their fellow Jews in fellowship, study, and worship. When they were expelled from the synagogues because of their expanded Jewish faith that included their understanding that Jesus was Messiah and Lord, they simply formed their own synagogues, which later came to be called churches.[31]

During the time of second-temple Judaism and the formation of the earliest Christian church, however, the synagogue was never viewed as a replacement for the home as the center for spiritual, social, and intellectual development. The family continued to be a temple where fellowship, study, and worship took place on a continuing daily basis and even more so on *Shabbat*. As a matter of fact, the Sabbath celebration of the earliest Christians was extended into the evening of the first day of the week (Saturday night) so that they celebrated fellowship, study, and worship on the evening of the first day of the week that preceded the morning of that day of the week in biblical tradition. From creation forward, from God's perspective, *"the evening* [first] and [then] *the morning* were the first day."[32]

Eventually, after the destruction of the temple in AD 70, when the sages of Israel observed the brokenheartedness of their people, they ruled that every home was to be viewed as a *mikdash me'at*, a mini-temple. As such, the home was formally recognized by the leaders of Israel as a small version of the ancient temple in Jerusalem. What had functioned for millennia without formalization was finally recognized and confirmed by Israel's spiritual leaders.

The sages based their declaration on the prophetic words that God had spoken to Israel through the prophet Ezekiel: "Although I have scattered [the Jews] among the countries, yet will I be to them as a little sanctuary in the countries where they shall come."[33] The Hebrew term that is correctly translated "little sanctuary" in Ezekiel's prophecy, מְעַט מִקְדָּשׁ (*mikdash me'at*). This is precisely the same term that has been applied to the Jewish home through the centuries and continues to be applied even to it to this day. While the sages also recognized the emergence of houses of learning in Babylon as another fulfillment of Ezekiel's prophecy,[34] they still understood that, fundamentally, God had purposed that the home and family would also be the fulfillment of God's prediction to his people.

The Hebrew word *mikdash* means "sanctuary." *Mikdash* comes from the word *kadash*, which means to be "holy" in the sense of being "consecrated" or "set apart." Both the tabernacle and the temple as sanctuaries were "set apart" exclusively for the worship of God. They were "holy" unto the Lord. Similarly, as a *mikdash me'at*, the home of each family in any worshipping community is "holy" unto the Lord, a consecrated and set-apart space whose focus is on God and his Word.

Because of the insight of the sages of Israel, who recognized that all of their religious exercises were based fundamentally in what God had designed for the family, the Jewish home has continued to be recognized as a *mikdash me'at*, a mini-temple. The one institution that God designed as foundational for relationship among his earthly children is to be replicated in each individual home around the world. In reality, the tabernacle and temple were merely extended manifestations of the home and extended applications of the functions of the home. The undeniable importance of the home as the center for spiritual development is clearly underscored by its formal recognition in the Jewish community as a temple in miniature.

A CASTLE OR A TEMPLE?

Most of the Western world has considered the home to be a castle. Indeed, a common dictum that has been used through the centuries says, "A man's home is his castle." Though this statement has served to underscore and reinforce the dominance of the male in the home and has contributed to the sad abuse of women in many, if not most, Western societies, the

idea behind the statement—that the home is a sacred space—
has solid support both from history and from the Holy Scriptures.

Over two millennia ago, the Roman philosopher and states-
man Cicero said, *"Quid est sanctius, quid omni religione munitius,
quam domus unius cujusque civium?"* ("What is more sacred, what
more strongly guarded by every holy feeling, than a man's own
home?").[35] This sacred, inviolable perspective on the home was
codified into law in seventeenth-century England by renowned
jurist Sir Edward Coke through his ruling that "an Englishman's
home is his castle, *et domus sua cuique est tutissimum refugium* [and
each man's home is his safest refuge]."[36] Later, in the eighteenth
century, William Blackstone reiterated this principle of English
common law by appealing to Cicero's dictum. He noted that
"the law of England has so particular and tender a regard to the
immunity of a man's house, that it stiles it his castle, and will
never suffer it to be violated with immunity."[37]

Since English common law, along with the Hebrew Scriptures, became the foundation of American law and tradition, the
idea of the sanctity of the home continued in the American
colonies. The term *man* was substituted for the term *Englishman*
so that the dictum became "A man's home is his castle." Every
man was given the right to defend his home in the same way that
an ancient lord would have defended his castle, and anyone who
dared to invade that space was subject to being killed without
any penalty.

While this perspective on the home became virtually all
pervasive, it was not a theme adopted by the international Jewish
community. Joseph Hertz explains: "The Jew's home has rarely
been his 'castle.' Throughout the ages it has been something far
higher—his sanctuary."[38] The Jewish people had a much higher
estimation of the value and importance of their homes. They
were not just castles designed for male dominance that were to

be defended against all intruders. They were instead temples, miniature versions of the ancient sanctuary that God commanded Moses to build as a habitation for the divine Spirit and of the temple that King David envisioned and his son Solomon built as the center of Jewish religious exercise.

Why would any family want a castle-home when they can have a temple-home? A castle is remote, cold, forbidding: a temple is open, warm, inviting. A castle is a fortified structure for military defense and separation: a temple is an open structure for public fellowship and worship. A castle is a symbol of power and wealth: a temple is a symbol of self-sacrifice and service. A castle is a place for pitched battles against enemies: a temple is a place for relationship with friends and family and reconciliation with enemies.

BACK TO THE BIBLE

Every Christian home should follow the example of the four-thousand-year-old tradition of the Hebrew, Israelite, and Jewish communities by becoming a genuine house of God, a temple in miniature. If true fellowship, study, and worship were conducted in each home on a continuing basis, the entire Christian community would be a much stronger institution. Public worship in congregational settings would become celebrations of what the Almighty had done in the context of each individual family in the community. Christians would then be living their faith not just for a few hours on the weekend but for seven days a week, and they would be living that faith where it really counts: in their families and in the marketplace and public arena.

If all the church can hear the call of the growing numbers of families that are transforming their homes into houses of God, perhaps over-institutionalized, over-programmed, performance-based Christianity can experience a rebirth of the original Christian experience. The impact on world societies would be earthshaking: "They who have turned the world upside down have come here also."[39]

[1] Genesis 3:8.

[2] Genesis 5:22.

[3] Hebrews 11:5.

[4] Genesis 6:2.

[5] Genesis 6:9.

[6] Genesis 6:8.

[7] Genesis 14:18-19.

[8] Sh'muel Ben Avraham, *Shem Mishmuel*, tr. Zvi Bevloski (South Field, MI: Targum Press, 1998), p. 35.

[9] Sarah Aranoff Tuchman and Sandra E. Rapoport, *The Passions of the Matriarchs* (Jersey City, NJ: KTAV Publishing House, 2004), p. 79.

[10] Genesis 18:1-10.

[11] Romans 4:11.

[12] Genesis 18:19; Micah 6:8.

[13] Exodus 12:8, 11, 22, paraphrased.

[14] Exodus 12:3, NIV.

[15] Exodus 12:14.

[16] Deuteronomy 6:21. God instructed the Israelites to tell their children, "*We* were slaves to Pharaoh in Egypt, and the LORD brought *us* from Egypt with a mighty hand."

[17] Exodus 19:6.

[18] Exodus 12:3, 6. In this case, the community (קָהָל—*kahal* in Hebrew) becomes the congregation (עֵדָה—*'edah*) when it is gathered for corporate worship, which includes three dynamics: fellowship, study, and prayer/worship.

[19] Exodus 18:17-24.

[20] Even though the camp of the Israelites moved when the divine cloud that marked the place of the sanctuary moved, the sanctuary was clearly designed to be with the people.

[21] Genesis 35:2.

[22] Exodus 16:15.

[23] 2 Samuel 6:14.

[24] 2 Samuel 6:20.

[25] Numbers 6:23.

[26] 2 Samuel 7:5-7.

[27] Psalm 137:2-4.

[28] ¹Israel was commanded to engage in corporate worship exercises in addition to their worship in the context of family. These were the convocations (calling together) which God required of them (cf. Leviticus 23:2). Exercises of family worship never exempted believers from the requirement to assemble together in the corporate sanctuary (Hebrews 10:25). It is in the context of community that worship is fully expressed and accountability is maintained. As a matter of fact, many of the most prominent prayers in the Jewish community cannot be prayed except in the company of ten men, the *minyan* or quorum for prayer. This is also why rabbis answer in terms of families, not individuals, when asked about the size of their congregations.

[29] Church as a spiritual entity was first manifest at Sinai. The Greek word that is translated "church" in English versions of the Scriptures is actually ἐκκλησία (*ekklesia*) in the Greek. The word *ekklesia* was used in the Septuagint Greek version of the

Hebrew Scriptures (the version most commonly used in the first-century Gentile church) to translate the Hebrew word קָהָל (*kahal*), which simply means "congregation." The *kahal* was the "church in the wilderness" to which Stephen alluded in Acts 7:38.

[30] Johnson Grant, *Sketches in Divinity* (London: Hatchard & Son, 1840), p. 399.

[31] Proof that the meetings of the Christians maintained the synagogal tradition of the Jews is seen in the fact that after the Day of Pentecost, the church was said to have "continued stedfast in the apostles' teaching, fellowship, and prayer" (Acts 2:42). Their teaching, fellowship, and prayer maintained the three functions of the synagogue. Additionally, some thirty years after the ascension of Jesus, James still referred to the corporate gatherings of the church among the "twelve tribes scattered abroad" (James 1:1) as "synagogues" (James 2:2).

[32] See Benjamin B. Babbit, ed., "Evening Communions and the Night of the Commandment," *The Church Monthly* (Boston: The Church Reading Room, 1868), vol. 14, pp. 175-177. Babbit points out that "[earliest] Christians began the first day of the week (our Saturday evening) with the *aagape* or feast of charity, continued their prayers, readings, and exhortations through the night, at least on special occasions, and kept the Saviour's dying memorial some time before they separated in the morning; the whole being a manifest imitation of that last night with His disciples; though the celebration of the Eucharist before daybreak seems to have had some reference also, in the minds of the early Fathers, to His having consecrated that hour by His rising from the tomb." Amazingly, this nineteenth-century interpretation is accurate whereas various other interpretations have the church celebrating communion after midnight on Monday! (See Hugh F. Pyle, *The Truth About the Church of Christ* [Murfreesboro, TN: Sword of the Lord Publishers, 1977], p. 74; Russell R. Standish and Colin D. Standish, *Pope's Letter and Sunday Laws* [Rapidan, VA: Hartland Publications, 1988], p. 10). This confusion results from the lack of simple understanding that the biblical day begins at sunset, not midnight or sunrise. Scripture is clear: "The evening and morning were the first day" (Genesis 1:5). The "first day of the week" celebration of the earliest Christians, then, was simply a continuation of their Sabbath celebration into the evening of the first day (Saturday night).

[33] Ezekiel 11:16.

[34] Talmud, *Megillah* 29a. See Sandor Scheiber, *Occident and Orient: A Tribute to the Memory of Alexander Scheiber* (Leiden: E. J. Brill, 1988), p. 211, n. 2.

[35] Marcus Tullius Cicero, *Ad Pontifices*, XLI, 109.

[36] Edward Coke, *The Institutes of the Lawes of England* (London: E & R Brook, 1787), p. 161.

[37] *William Blackstone's Commentaries on the Laws of England, Facsimile of the First Edition of 1765-1769* (Chicago: University of Chicago Press, 1979), vol. 4, p. 223.

[38] Joseph H. Hertz, ed., *A Book of Jewish Thoughts* (New York: Oxford University Press, 1920), p. 11.

[39] Acts 17:6.

Chapter 4

The Domestic Priesthood

LEADING THE FAMILY TEMPLE

When one fully understands that the family home is a temple, a house of God, then it becomes very reasonable to consider the roles of priesthood that are to be fulfilled in a fully functioning domestic temple. If the home is truly a house of God—and, indeed, the basis for all other manifestations of the house of God—then the activities that should be transpiring in the home are of such a sacred nature that they require that parents fulfill priestly functions that elevate experience of the home from the mundane to the sublime.

Dayle Friedman gives a beautiful, succinct summation of the Jewish home that should by all rights also describe every Christian home. "One's home is one's Temple, the marital partners assume the role of the priest, their table becomes the altar on which they offer the sacrifice of their hearts, and all that goes on within that tabernacle, including human relationships, has the potential to be holy."[1] If all Christian families considered their homes to be houses of God as the Jews clearly do, it would be easy for them to recognize the roles and functions of priesthood that are incumbent upon them so that they can, indeed, transfer everything that properly transpires within their family temple into an act of holiness unto the Lord. This Jewish understanding of home life is clearly what Paul, who was first a Jewish rabbi and then a Christian apostle, meant when he said, "Whatever you do, do all to the glory of God."[2]

Often Christians think that only what is done in the church or in some function of the church can be done to the glory of God. Everything else, including home life, is part of the secular realm. There was no such dichotomy between the spiritual and the secular, however, in Paul's mind because he knew from his rabbinic training that everything in life, especially in the family temple, is holy unto the Lord. The truth is that everything—"whatever you do"—should bring glory to God, especially everything that is done in the home as a family temple.

In order for the home to carry out the functions of a temple, some form of priesthood must be manifest. In Israel's sanctuaries, God ordained the tribe of Levi and more specifically the sons of Aaron to fulfill this role.[3] The functions of the priesthood were threefold: to make sacrifices for sin, to teach God's Word, and to lead in corporate worship. Each of these three functions remained fully operative when the first-century New Covenant community emerged.

Priesthood was fulfilled when Jesus himself entered into the Most Holy Place in heaven once and for all time, offering his own blood to atone for all the sins of humanity, past, present, and future.[4] Though all will not believe and will not, therefore, be saved from their sins; nevertheless, the provision was made in that one event of redemption to atone for all human sin.

For the subsequent believers in Jesus as Messiah, the sacrificial role of priesthood under the Sinai covenant was reversed. Whereas the Aaronic priesthood had offered men's sacrifices for sin to God, the Christian priesthood of all believers has offered Jesus, God's only sacrifice for sin, to men, saying, "Be reconciled to God."[5] By being the witnesses that Jesus commissioned them to be,[6] this royal priesthood literally sacrifices the gospel of God, offering it to humanity for salvation and the forgiveness of sins.[7] The sacrificial role of priesthood for the family priests has always been the same as for all other Christian believers, both laity and leaders.

Then, from time immemorial, the leaders of both the community and the family were commissioned to teach the Word of God. This role of priesthood was used to underscore God's instructions for humanity both in their own lives as living examples and in continually reinforcing the responsibility of individuals and the community of faith to be obedient to God's instructions. In the Christian community, the same function continued in both family and congregational priesthoods as a part of the priesthood of all believers. The priestly role of family and community leaders was fulfilled in teaching the Word of God.

Finally, the Christian leaders and heads of household, like the priests of old, were to lead in acts of worship and praise to the Almighty. All believers everywhere are to do all that they do to the glory of God,[8] to offer sacrifices of praise and thanksgiving to his name,[9] and to ascribe greatness and honor to the Most High God. When a truly Hebraic understanding of worship is present in the church, the exercise of reverence both in congregational and familial settings is continual.[10] It is expanded beyond the once-a-week experience of most Christianity to a daily exercise in the family temple.

In the New Covenant community, the three functions of priesthood are carried out on four levels. The first is the High Priest, Jesus, who atones for sins, teaches righteousness, and engenders worship. Jesus is the High Priest in the temple or sanctuary in heaven.[11] The second level of priesthood is manifest in the leaders whom God has positioned to provide oversight and protection for the community of faith in all of its various levels of manifestation. These are the leaders or priests in the spiritual temple,[12] the congregation. The third level is the priesthood in the home, with the head of each household charged with the responsibility of instructing the family in ways of righteousness and leading in worship. Parents are leaders or priests in the temple of the home. The fourth level is the priesthood of all human beings and more particularly of all believers. Since every human body is designed to be a temple for God,[13] anyone can function as a priest to approach God for himself to obtain the forgiveness of sins and acceptance into the family of God. The only mediator is the High Priest himself.[14] Likewise, all believers who have come to faith in God function as priests on a continuing basis,[15] having direct access to the High Priest for the forgiveness of sins, for understanding God's instructions for humankind, and for direct worship of the Heavenly Father.

In Christian history, it is the third level of priesthood—the family priesthood—that has been most neglected. This is the area where restoration is needed for the health of the church in general and for the well-being of individuals in particular. Virtually all of the church has been very careful to give preeminence in all things to Jesus the High Priest. A proper understanding that priesthood extends to all believers has also been prominent in much of Christianity, particularly Protestantism. Additionally, Christians have generally manifest a biblically mandated show of respect for leaders in the church who have been chosen to lead the faith community in things pertaining to God. In the process, however, the organized church and virtually all believers have neglected the important level of priesthood that should function in every home.

It is a simple fact of history that family worship predated corporate worship. The community—whether the church or the synagogue—was birthed from the family, not vice versa. As a matter of fact, when corporate exercises emerged, they were merely extensions of family worship for an extended family or community. This in no way obviates or minimizes the importance of or the need for organized approaches to corporate worship. This is clearly mandated in Scripture which specifically says, "Forsake not the assembling of yourselves together."[16] This and other passages of Scripture do not, however, replace the family temple, which continues to be a long-neglected vital element in the life of the corporate worshipping community that Christians call "church." The biblical family always has been and always will be the locus for growth and development of the whole human person, socially, educationally, and spiritually. If the family is first a mini-temple, then the community is a mini-temple in the expanded dimension for which it was designed. The community as congregation merely expands the functions of the family.

If the home is a temple, then it follows that priesthood must be represented in the home. A temple without a functioning priestly office and ritual is nothing but an empty shell, for the sole reason for a temple to exist is to facilitate the worship exercises that pertain to the physical structure. In order to make a home a temple with a functioning priestly office, however, one must have a clear understanding of the principles and practice of priesthood. All the functions of the priesthood in the ancient temple in Jerusalem, therefore, must also be manifest in the home just as they are in the corporate community of believers. The form, detail, and application may vary, but the principles must be faithfully replicated.

The head of each household should function in a priestly role toward the rest of the family. The firstborn sons of ancient Israel belonged to the Lord.[17] Apparently, God intended that the firstborn of each family would make up the priesthood; however, they were redeemed and replaced by the Levites.[18] Until that time, however, parents shared the priestly function in the

home. This order still remains for the proper operation of the
Christian home as a family temple.

FATHERS AS PRIESTS IN THE HOME

Because the church has removed priesthood functions from
the home, it has largely emasculated its male members. The
church has relegated most of the males in society to a position
of being engaged in "secular" work and, therefore, of not doing
God's work. For this reason, most males do not see a role for
themselves in the church. Christianity has come to recognize as
"men of God" only those who are fulfilling roles of public
ministry. The rest of men are seen as laborers whose function
it is to support their families and the organized church.

The truth is that all men who are believers are "men of
God," sharing equally with the "men of the cloth" this title and
function. Work itself is worship,[19] and there is no legitimate
bifurcation separating spiritual work and secular work. Indeed,
any attempt to segregate the "spiritual" from the "secular" is a
false dichotomy, for there is no such thing as "secular": everything is spiritual.[20] All work is spiritual because it fulfills the
divine command, "Six days shall you work."[19] It should come as
no surprise, therefore, that one of the words for worship in
Hebrew is also the word for work: עֲבֹדָה (abodah). The church
desperately needs to close the centuries-old clergy–laity gap by
understanding that all of its members are men and women of
God, not just those who are employed professionally by the
church. It also needs to restore the biblically Hebraic understanding that husbands and fathers have a God-given responsibility to be "men of God" in their own homes, leading their
families in things pertaining to God.

Every man's work must also be understood from a biblical
perspective as being a "ministry." The work of ministry is not the
exclusive province of those who are gifted to lead the corporate

community of believers. It is a function of every man and every woman. The "ministry" of work in every man's life must, however, be emphasized because work was assigned to the man after the fall of Adam and remains man's chief source of self-identity and self-worth.[21]

When all Christian men come to understand that their work is God's work and that it is a ministry, they are elevated to a state of equality with those men who are leaders in the church. There are no longer two tiers of manhood and male worth, clergy and laity. There are simply different functions, different gifts, and different administrations. Whereas some are gifted to teach, preach, counsel, or lead in worship, all are gifted with the ministry of working to provide for themselves and their families.

When all work is seen as worship and as a ministry, all men can emerge from church-inflicted emasculation to assume the roles of leadership for which they were designed by God to accomplish. Since they are doing God's work throughout the day, they can come to their homes and continue God's work as priestly leaders of their own families. Wives and children can find in their own homes the righteous man who demonstrates the qualities extolled in Psalm 1 and Psalm 112. Families can delight in the priestly leadership of their head of household rather than reserving religious respect and awe exclusively for ordained ministry and church leaders. If this were done universally, much of the counseling load of the clergy would simply disappear.

Men who have recovered this accurate biblical and Hebraic understanding of their own roles do not have to control their wives and children in abusive domination-submission codependencies in order to gain the respect they feel they need. They realize that they are men of God, responsible for exhibiting the qualities of love and tender mercy that Christ manifests toward his bride, the church, and that God himself continually extends toward all of his children. Assuming the role of priest in the home places an awesome responsibility on a husband and father. He cannot be a dictator with everyone serving his whims. He must be a facilitator, in love serving both his wife and his children and setting an example of right and generous conduct that those little ones who will replace him on earth can follow. He must sacrifice his own ambitions and "needs" for the sake of love for his family in the same manner in which Jesus gave his life out of love for the church.[22]

MOTHERS AS PRIESTS IN THE HOME

For centuries, virtually all Christians have believed that women could not possibly have any priestly role in any aspect of the church. Since the ministry of the church has been seen as a priesthood and since women were never involved in the priesthood of the Israelite economy, women have been excluded from being "priests," even in the home. If any role of priesthood was permissible in the home, it was restricted to the father. Many theologians believed (and still do to this day) that since Jesus was a male when he was incarnate on earth, only men can be "Christomorphic," that is, bearing the image of Christ, especially as a priest.

In the beginning, however, it is clear that both Adam and Eve functioned as priests in their garden home. Jacques Doukhan points out that the very fact that God himself clothed Adam and Eve after their sin with the skin or hide of an animal is proof that even in their fallen state, God appointed them to roles of priesthood. "The rare occasions where God clothes humans in the Old Testament always concerned the dressing of priest," Doukhan notes.[23] Indeed, the use of the Hebrew words *kotnot* ("garments") and *labash* ("to clothe") when the text says that "God made garments of skin and clothed them" directly parallels the terminology used to describe God's specifications for the priests' garments.[24] This fact led Doukhan to conclude that "by bestowing on Adam and Eve the skin of the sin offering, a gift strictly reserved to priests, the Genesis story implicitly recognizes Eve as a priest alongside Adam."[25]

It is entirely likely that women were excluded from the Aaronic priesthood because of the predominance of priestesses in the religious exercises of the heathen nations that surrounded the Israelite nation and because of the intense sexual license that was associated with the worship of the idols of those peoples. In God's effort to insulate his chosen people from the practices of the idolaters, he restricted their involvement in various activities that were common to those nations, especially to the public worship of those false deities.

When it came to the home, however, it was clear that women fulfilled roles that were reserved to the priesthood, including that of teaching—in this case, the teaching of children in the home. Teaching was a function of the priesthood: "You shall carefully observe whatever the levitical priests teach you,"[26] God commanded the Israelites. Anyone who engages in teaching is, therefore, fulfilling at least one aspect of the role of priesthood. When it comes to mothers in the home, Solomon was very clear about this role and responsibility, noting twice: "Do not forsake your mother's teaching."[27] Wives and mothers, therefore, have a significant priestly responsibility in the domestic temple.

They can and should fulfill the New Covenant roles of priesthood by sacrificing the gospel of the kingdom, saying to their children, "Be reconciled to God." They should lead in prayer. They should bless their husbands and children. And they should teach their children the ways of the Lord. In the family temple, therefore, there is a family priesthood—husband and wife, father and mother—who are used of God to lead the family in fellowship, study, and worship.

[1] Dayle A. Friedman, *Jewish Pastoral Care: A Practical Handbook from Traditional and Con-*

temporary Sources (Woodstock, VT: Jewish Lights Publications, 2005), p. 247.

[2] 1 Corinthians 10:31.

[3] Hebrews 7:11.

[4] Hebrews 9:12.

[5] 2 Corinthians 5:20.

[6] Acts 1:8.

[7] Romans 15:16. This passage is accurately rendered, "That I should be the liturgist of Jesus Christ, sacrificing the gospel of God."

[8] Colossians 3:17; 2 Corinthians 4:15.

[9] 1 Peter 2:5; Hebrews 13:16.

[10] 1 Thessalonians 5:17-18

[11] Hebrews 9:24.

[12] 1 Peter 2:5.

[13] 1 Corinthians 6:19.

[14] 1 Timothy 2:5; Hebrews 8:6; 9:15.

[15] 1 Peter 2:9.

[16] Hebrews 10:25.

[17] Exodus 13:13.

[18] Jeremy Benstein, *The Way into Judaism and the Environment* (Woodstock, VT: Jewish Lights Publishing, 2006), pp. 47-48. Benstein points out that the Hebrew word *abodah* means both worship and work while the English word *work* comes from the same source as the word *worship*. See also Marvin R. Wilson, *Our Father Abraham: Jewish Roots of the Christian Faith* (Grand Rapids, MI: Wm. B. Eerdmans Publishing Co., 1989), p. 310.

[19] Noel A. Humphrey, *Gathering the Next Generation: Essays on the Formation and Ministry of GenX Priests* (Harrisburg, PA: Morehouse Publishing, 2000), p. 72. Also David Claerbaut, *Faith and Learning on the Edge: A Bold New Look at Religion in Higher Education* (Grand Rapids, MI: Zondervan Publishing, 2004), p. 112.

[20] Exodus 20:9.

[21] Genesis 3:17-19.

[22] Ephesians 5:25.

[23] Jacques B. Doukhan, "Women Priests in Israel: A Case for Their Absence," in *Women in Ministry: Biblical and Historical Perspectives*, ed. Nancy Vyhmeister (Berrien Springs, MI: Andrews University Press, 1998), p. 36.

[24] Exodus 40:14.

[25] Doukhan, p. 37.

[26] Deuteronomy 24:8.

[27] Proverbs 1:8; 6:20.

Chapter 5

The Domestic Church

THE FAMILY AS "CHURCH"

Original Christianity was simply an extension and full manifestation of the model of community interaction, study, and worship that had developed during the Babylonian exile and had become normative for the society into which Jesus and the apostles were born. The synagogue (meeting or assembly) was the dominant functioning expression of daily and weekly exercises of worship throughout Israel and in the Jewish diaspora during the first century. The synagogues were not buildings; they were meetings of people. By this time, Judaism had adopted the Greek word συναγωγή (*sunagoge*), meaning "meeting or assembly," to describe this manifestation of community.

Though the temple and its priesthood continued to maintain an important role in the everyday lives of the Jewish community in the time of Jesus, the temple cultus increasingly shared many roles of worship with the synagogue. It was in this synagogue matrix that Jesus and his apostles lived their lives as part of a dynamic Jewish community. It was in this setting that they worshiped and expressed their devotion to God. The Scriptures affirm that Jesus joined his fellow Jews in the synagogue on the Sabbath day "as his custom was."[1] Paul and the apostles maintained the same customs.[2] Even thirty years after the resurrection of Jesus, Christian corporate worshipping communities were still being called "synagogues"[3] by the apostle James.

The Jewish people had discovered during the Babylonian captivity that they could worship God without the temple and without a functioning priesthood. When Nebuchadnezzar destroyed the temple, the people simply elevated to greater prominence the worship exercises that had originally been centered in their homes and extended families before the priesthood and its attendant cultus had been introduced. Meetings sprang up in Jewish communities right in the midst of the Babylonian captivity, as dutiful, worshipping Jewish families expressed their public devotion to God even in the midst of their enslavement. The foundation of a tradition that has since transcended more than two millennia emerged. The synagogue was born.

The earliest synagogues were simply extensions into community-wide models of family worship exercises. First the Jews worshipped God as families; then families came together in communities to worship corporately, thereby multiplying the worship dynamic. The synagogue was never the model that was then replicated in the home. The family temple was rather duplicated and expanded in the synagogue. As always, the family was the foundational unit and the model for the corporate community.

Two of the functions of priesthood were immediately manifest in these meetings. First, there was teaching of the Word of God. Second, corporate prayers were offered in the name of all of Israel. Eventually, prayers, Torah study, and acts of charity and piety even came to be viewed as being legitimate substitutes for the temple sacrifices.[4] This was especially true after the destruction of the temple in AD 70, when the rabbis at Yavneh recognized what their fellow Jews—the prophets and Jesus and his apostles—had already come to understand, that worship was not restricted to the temple and involved much more than sacrifices and offerings.[5]

In the midst of this passion for study and worship, however, a new social order was also emerging. The synagogue became a societal meeting dynamic, a mechanism for social interaction, a true place of meeting for fellowship. It became, in effect, a Jewish community center. Biblical human interaction provides for social relationship as well as for study and worship. A worshipping community that neglects any of these three dynamics is, therefore, deficient.

Social relationship, study, and worship became the three functions of the synagogue. Eventually, these functions were adopted as names for the synagogue which came to be described as a *Beth Knesset* (House of Meeting),[6] a *Beth Midrash* (House of Study), and a *Beth Tefillah* (House of Prayer). In the latter case, the prophetic description of the temple itself[7] became a term that identified the synagogue. Except for carrying out the sacrificial system, the synagogue had become a mini-temple (*mikdash me'at*) in itself. Indeed, its three functions replicated the distinct areas and furnishings of Israel's wilderness tabernacle as well as the three compartments of Abraham and Sarah's tent.

It should come as no surprise, then, that the three synagogal functions were the features of earliest Christianity which developed from the matrix of second-temple Judaism. Jesus and his disciples were not engaged in establishing an alternative priesthood or a new religion for their Jewish family. They simply continued in continuity with the religion and the systems in which they had been reared and with which they were totally comfortable. There was no lurching demand for an innovative religious form or substance. They were Jews, their religion was Judaism, and they abandoned neither their ethnicity nor their religion.

The disciples sought to make their understanding that in the person of Jesus the Messianic expectations of their Jewish family had been fully realized and that God's promise to bring salvation to Israel and the world had brought completion and fulfillment to their ancient system of praise, worship, and service. They knew from his own testimony that Jesus did not come to destroy the Torah or the prophets but to fulfill them.[8] Large portions of the first-century Jewish community in Israel and abroad came to share this prophetic insight. What eventually came to be thought of as a Gentile religion was in reality one of the most dominant forms of first-century Judean and Galilean second-temple Judaism.

THE SYNAGOGAL MINI-TEMPLE MODEL

The synagogal model was perfectly manifest in the first days of the empowered congregation that eventually came to be known as the *ekklesia* (church). The disciples' dynamism and impact upon their fellow citizens of Israel was said to have been the result of the fact that they continued in the apostles' "teaching," in "fellowship" (including breaking of bread), and in "prayers,"[9] these three, nothing more and nothing less. Of course, these were precisely the three functions of and names for the synagogue. Since the earliest Christian believers were steadfast Jews, they continued to function in a community as a *Beth Midrash* (apostolic teaching), as a *Beth Knesset* (fellowship or social interaction), and as a *Beth Tefillah* (prayers). As they continued in this tradition, "the LORD added daily to the congregation those who were saved," as many as 5,000 in one day! "Myriads" (tens of thousands) of Jewish Pharisees[10] and large numbers of temple priests[11] openly professed their faith in Jesus as Messiah. Increasing numbers of scholars have come to recognize that the number of Jews who believed in Jesus as Messiah during the first century was significantly larger than had been previously thought, with some suggesting that by the end of the first century at least 100,000 Jews were part of the emerging Christian community.[12]

Another significant development in the earliest church was

the fact that the community "broke bread from house to house."[13] The breaking of bread was an ongoing exercise of fellowship within the Jewish community that has been described by theologians as "table fellowship."[14] People gathered around the tables in their homes and shared food and fellowship, study and worship. The earliest Christian synagogue was a house church.[15] Corporate worship was first a family exercise in which other members of the larger community were invited to share food and fellowship in a purely social activity of community building. Then came the exercises of studying God's Word together and joining in corporate prayers. There was no temple, no cathedral, no church, not even a chapel. There were only homes! Family worship was the focus of the earliest congregation of Jesus, the church of Christ.

Leaders emerged from among those who were the heads of households, not from a professional clergy class. The earliest trans-local leaders were the apostles themselves who had been trained at the feet of Jesus in the community-renewal movement that much later came to be called "church." The apostles did not, however, see themselves as a replacement for the temple priesthood. As a matter of fact, they continued to worship at the temple[16] and even decades after Jesus' ascension still recognized the authority of the temple priesthood and engaged in temple ritual. Paul, the apostle to the Gentiles, submitted himself to temple purification rites,[17] and James was recognized as "the Just" by the traditional Jewish leaders because he faithfully observed the Torah within the context of the Jerusalem Jewish community.[18]

CHRISTIAN CONTINUITY

Neither Jesus nor his apostles intended to create a new religion called "Christianity." They sought only to reform the religion of their ancestors, the religion that God himself had authored at Sinai and through Jesus had perfected at Calvary. They were not attempting to establish a new social or religious order that they

called "church." They *were* continuing in the rich, centuries-old tradition of the Jewish synagogue and within the overarching parameters of what by that time had come to be called "Judaism."[19] More
than three decades after Pentecost, the local manifestations of the
church were still being called "synagogues" at least among the Jewish Christian diaspora.[20] The word *church*, along with all of its attendant implications, was a Medieval misinterpretation of what the
Greek word ἐκκλησία (*ekklesia*) and its Hebrew counterpart קָהָל
(*kahal*) meant to Jesus and the apostles. The word *church* that
appears in most English versions of the Bible should always have
been translated "congregation" or "community."

Since the earliest leaders of the church in no way viewed
themselves as a new priesthood set apart from the rest of the
believing community (as were the Aaronic priests), they continued as laypersons and as servants of the people. The fundamental title that was applied to all the leaders, including Jesus himself,[21]
was διακονέω (*diakoneo*), meaning "servant" or "minister."[22] Nowhere in the record of the Apostolic Scriptures did Christian
leaders bear the title of "priest." They certainly functioned in
priestly roles to be sure, but they did so only in the context of
synagogal worship, not in the context of temple worship. They
fulfilled the priestly responsibilities of teaching and leading in
worship; however, they considered themselves, and were viewed
by others, as be servants in the truest synagogal sense. As servants, they were apostles, prophets, evangelists, pastors, and
teachers,[23] but never "priests."

God's intention from the beginning had always been that all
of Israel would be a "kingdom of priests."[24] Each Israelite was
to function as a priest with access to God, first for himself, then
for his family, and finally for the community. When Jesus fulfilled forever the sacrificial and liturgical system employed in the
tabernacle and in the temple, he became High Priest of a new
priesthood of all believers, the "royal priesthood" which Peter

described. [25] In order for Jesus to be a priest, however, the priesthood had to revert from the Aaronic order to its original order. This was the priesthood that was employed by God when he made Melchizedek, the king of Salem, the priest of the Most High God at the time when the Abrahamic faith and religion emerged. [26] God's eternal High Priest was his first and only begotten Son. [27] His priesthood was based in his being the first begotten among many brethren, [28] the head of the family of God. The continuing priesthood of believers was based in its service to the family and the extended family and in roles of leadership in home, synagogue, and community.

The principle of the priesthood was manifest in the most ancient times with the head of each household functioning as a priest. It was the responsibility of the head of each family to lead the family in matters of social and spiritual interaction, in matters of study, and in matters of worship and prayer. The home was the center for every aspect of life.

RENEWING THE FAMILY TEMPLE

Much like Solomon's temple, the family temple has suffered destruction both as a conceptual idea and as a practical reality. Something akin to Babylon has overwhelmed this ancient, biblically Hebraic formula, replacing it almost exclusively with corporate sanctuaries and public worship. Now it is time for a restoration to take place akin to that of the time of Ezra and Nehemiah, of Joshua and Zerubbabel, of Haggai and Zechariah.

The home that has for so long been relegated to a position of relative unimportance as a mere social convention must now be restored to the position of honor that it had in biblical times as a family temple. In a day of increasing onslaughts against this, the fundamental societal unit, it is imperative that both the Jewish and Christian communities hold up the biblical standard of family identity in the face of the violence directed against the home by the enemies of faith. The family must be restored as the center for social, educational, and spiritual development. Anything less spells disaster for both church and society at large.

The idea of a fully functioning domestic temple runs cross current to most historical Christian ecclesiology which has generally viewed the church as either functioning around a bishop (Orthodox) or pope (Catholic) or as a congregation (most of Protestantism). In each case, worship experiences have been thought to require a priest, bishop, or minister and a congregation.[29] Jesus, however, made it clear that "where two or three are gathered in my name, I am in their midst,"[30] and he gave no indication that one of these two had to be a priest or a minister. Where Christ is present, the church is fully manifest, and this can be with only two people, husband and wife, or the head of household and the children in the case of a single-parent family.

Perhaps Jesus' statement was designed to circumvent the rabbinic requirement that a *minyan* (quorum) of ten men be present for a functioning *Beth Tefillah* to be constituted so that collective prayers could be prayed.[31] Jesus' teaching clearly supports the truth that the "church" exists when at least two people are gathered in his name, and this is precisely what occurs when any family gathers in his name in their family temple. The "church," therefore, is fully manifest in each family mini-temple.

Each family must view its home as a mini-temple in which all the functions of biblical community life have their beginnings and are fully manifest. This restoration will restore a God-consciousness to both the church and society that will transcend the nominal Christian experience. It will return the family of God to a face-to-face relationship of walking with God, the spiritual experience that predated and supersedes both Judaism and Christianity. In effect, it will be Eden renewed in the family temple.

Adopting these biblically Hebraic views will empower families to make their homes such powerful sanctuaries of blessing that extended family, friends, and even strangers will welcome the experience of warmth and joy that inclusion in this circle of loving affirmation provides. Restoring familial social interaction, teaching, and worship, the home will become one of the church's most effective agents for evangelism and community development. The church will multiply itself by the number of its families,[32] and the kingdom of God will advance through the domestic temple, the family sanctuary.

Perhaps a church impoverished by the loss of its Hebraic heritage and dessicated by dry rationalism void of the Holy Spirit can learn a lesson proposed by Baruch HaLevi and Ellen Frankel when they spoke of the role of the Spirit in their own Jewish faith in this manner: "If *Ruakh* [Holy Spirit] is to return to Judaism, it will only do so once we start thinking of our temples, our synagogues, and our shuls in terms other than as institutions, organizations, or buildings. Rather, the spirit will animate our religion once again when we reclaim the language of the home speaking to the comfort, nurturing, nuance, and intimacy of that sacred space."[33] Amen! May it be so!

[1] Luke 4:16.

[2] Acts 13:14, 42, 44; 18:4.

[3] James 2:2. James uses the Greek word συναγωγή (*sunagoge*) to describe the Christian assemblies. Virtually all English translations render *sunagoge* as "meeting" or "assembly," both of which are correct. The translators, however, engage in a massive inconsistency when they translate the precise same word συναγωγή (*sunagoge*) as "synagogue" when the texts speak the meetings of the Jews (John 18:20; Acts 14:1; 17:1, 10, 17) and of the meetings of Satan (Revelation 2:9). Apparently the translators agree that Jews and Satan can had synagogues but Christians cannot possibly have had synagogues (because eveyrone knows that they had "churches"); therefore, they translate the Greek word *sunagoge* in James 2:2 as "meeting" or "assembly." Only NJB, BBE, and NJB translate *sunagoge* consistently with the rest of the text of the Apostolic Scriptures as "synagogue."

[4] John 4:21-24; Hosea 6:6; Mark 12:33; Hebrews 10:5-6; 1 Peter 2:5.

[5] W. D. Davies, Louis Finkelstein, Steven T. Katz, *The Cambridge History of Judaism, Volume 4, The Late Roman-Rabbinic Period* (2006), vol. 4, p. 941.

[6] An important part of the *Beth Knesset* was the *Beth Din*, the house of judgment. Justice was dispensed in Israel in the context of the community meeting (*knesset*). The *Beth Din*, however, was not considered to be a fourth function of the synagogue.

[7] Isaiah 56:7.

[8] Matthew 5:17-18.

[9] Acts 2:42.

[10] Acts 21:20.

[11] Acts 6:7.

[12] Rodney Stark, noted in Michael L. Brown, *Answering Jewish Objections to Jesus: Volume 4: New Testament Objections* (Grand Rapids, MI: Baker Book House, 2007), p. 183.

[13] Acts 2:46.

[14] Michael F. Bird, *Jesus and the Origins of the Gentile Mission* (London: T & T Clark International, 1988), p. 104. See also Arthur A. Jus, *The Ongoing Feast: Table Fellowship and Eschatology at Emmaus* (Collegeville, NM: The Liturgical Press, 1993).

[15] Acts 2:46; 12:12; 16:40; Romans 16:3-5; Colossians 4:15; Philemon 1:2. See Joseph H. Hellerman, *The Ancient Church as Family* (Minneapolis, MN: Augsburg Fortress Press, 2001), p. 225.

[16] Acts 3:1; 22:17.

[17] Acts 21:26. Paul submitted to the rites of purification in the temple to prove that he had not violated the laws of God as he had been charged.

[18] James was revered by the traditional Jewish community because of his faithfulness to the Torah. See Jacobus De Voragine, *The Golden Legend: Readings on the Saints* (Princeton, NJ: Princeton University Press, 1993), vol. 1, p. 271.

[19] Galatians 1:13-14. Here Paul describes experiences from his life before his Damascus Road experience, using the Greek word Ἰουδαϊσμός (*Ioudaismos*), literally "Judaism," saying, "I was advancing in Judaism beyond many of my contemporaries. . . . being extremely zealous for my ancestral traditions" (NASB).

[20] James 2:2. See note 3 above.

[21] Romans 15:8.

[22] Ephesians 3:7.

[23] Ephesians 4:11.

[24] Exodus 19:6.

[25] 1 Peter 2:9.

[26] Hebrews 5:6-10.

[27] Hebrews 1:6; John 1:14.

[28] Romans 8:29.

[29] Matthew 18:20.

[30] The Catholic Church teaches that a priest can celebrate the eucharist with or without a congregation.

[31] This has been called in Judaism the *minyan*, which, in effect, is a quorum for prayer. The rabbinic requirement was originally for ten people (men and women) to be present; however, it was changed to limit the participants to men. The idea of a *minyan* was based on the instance where Abraham asked God to spare Sodom and Gomorrah if "ten" righteous people could be found there (Genesis 18:32). It is also based on the fact that the "ten spies" were termed "the congregation" in Numbers 14:27 and the ten sons of Jacob who went into Egypt were called "the congregation" in Genesis 42:5.

[32] Success in most churches today is measured by membership or attendees. Interestingly enough, when asked about how many "members" are in a particular Jewish synagogue, the rabbi will invariably respond not by giving a number of members but rather a number of *families*!

[33] Baruch HaLevi and Ellen Frankel, *Revolution of Jewish Spirit: How to Revive Ruakh in Your Spiritual Life, Transform Your Synagogue & Inspire Your Jewish Community* (Woodstock, VT: Jewish Lights Publishing, 2012), p. 66.

Chapter 6

The Family Altar

DISCOVERING AND USING YOUR FAMILY ALTAR

In historic Christianity, there has been little concern for a "family altar," for the entire concept of altars was connected with the formal public worship that was carried out in chapels, churches, and cathedrals by members of the priesthoods or clergy of various denominations. It has been widely believed that only such clergy professionals were qualified to attend at the altar and to carry out worship exercises, including sacraments of the church. Even with the advent of Protestantism beginning in the sixteenth century, the virtual wall of separation between clergy and laity was perpetuated in most communions. If there were concerns about a "family altar," they were developed and expressed in terms of the prayer life of the individual.

In recent times, there has been much discussion about the need to have a "family altar" in Christian homes. Many have wondered how to create such an altar and where it should be situated. Various suggestions have been made. Again, however, the primary context of the idea of a family altar has been that of having a designated place and perhaps time for prayer in the home.

The truth is, however, that every home already has a family altar. And its functions are wide and varied and contribute to the spiritual and social welfare of the entire family on an ongoing basis. The altar in every home is the table around which the family gathers for meals. Though not generally understood in Christian circles, this is a truth that is anchored in the words of Holy Scripture and in the earliest tradition of the Christian church.

When Christianity emerged from the matrix of biblical and second-temple Judaism, the tradition of the family altar was brought forward intact from its ancient background, and it was a distinct part of the understanding that the home was a temple in miniature. The logic was perfect: if the home was a temple, then it was certain that it must have had an altar.

In Jewish homes, the table has always been more than an appliance for dispensing and consuming food. It has been an altar. As a matter of fact, the family table has been considered to be parallel with the altar on which the sacrifices were offered in Israel's ancient sanctuaries, both in the tabernacle in the wilderness and in the temple in Jerusalem. This comparison was established biblically when the Prophet Malachi described the altar in the temple altar as a *shulchan* (table).[1] If God's altar was his table, the sages reasoned, then man's table must also be an altar. This is why Paul, the rabbi from Tarsus, argued that one could not partake of the Lord's *table* and the table of demons,[2] contrasting the tables in the house churches where believers shared communion with the altars in the pagan temples where the pantheon of Greek gods were worshipped.

Both the ancient Jewish understanding and the earliest Christian view of the table as an altar clearly establishes the sanctity of the home and its function as a temple with the table as its family altar. The biblical idea that the table is an altar underscores the fact that the home is, indeed, a temple. It is not simply a mundane domestic site where family members relate to each other on material levels. It is a holy site where the family gathers around the table and experiences interrelationality on a high spiritual level, and what takes place around the table is expanded to every aspect of family life so that everything, in reality, becomes a spiritual activity.

Wendy Mogel accurately describes the high value that is placed on the table in the Jewish home: "Our dining table with our children is an altar. It has the potential to be the holiest spot on the planet. In Jewish tradition, there are rules designed to help us sanctify all our daily enterprises, from the way we treat our spouses to the way we treat our children. . . . There are rules for reproof, for praise, for greeting in the morning and going to sleep at night, because in Jewish tradition each of these activities is holy."[3]

What is true for the Jewish family table can and should be true for the Christian family table. It is an altar for sharing both food and the word of God. In this context, even the food that is consumed by the family is eaten in a spiritual context that gives glory to God. This follows from the continuing biblical principle that "one does not live on bread alone," an idea that is confirmed in both the Hebrew and Apostolic Scriptures.[4] Every loaf of bread that is consumed in the home where the table is an altar dedicated to God takes on greater dimensions of purpose and reality. It becomes a spiritual action where minds are turned from hunger to thankfulness to God as the only one who "brings forth bread from the earth," as the Jewish *ha-motzi* blessing says.

Unfortunately in a large portion of modern homes, the table is little more than a feeding trough. Grace is rarely said at the table, and in more and more households, the family almost never gathers as a unit around the table. The table—or even more simply just the refrigerator or microwave—has become little more than a vending machine in a transportation terminal. Everyone grabs a bite in insolated and silent anonymity and quickly moves on. What few words that are exchanged are yelled over the din of private music piped in through earphones that virtually silence all competition or over the roar of television's mindless, inane laugh tracks.

This lack of respect for the sanctity of the family table was graphically illustrated in a radio commercial designed to sell furniture. When the delivery men were told to place the refrigerator in the den next to the television, they wondered, "Won't that make it hard to cook?" The homeowner replied reassuringly, "Of course not; one of the slots in the home entertainment center is reserved for the microwave!" This is just one example of the paradigm shift in relationship to the family activity of eating together. Eating has become utterly utilitarian with no thought to the spiritual significance of the act, especially in the context of the family.

Even if the family on occasion eats together, little thought is given to the sacredness of the occasion or of using the time to affirm familial relationships and to strengthen commitment to God. In the modern world, success and pleasure have become the supreme pursuits, the gods to which homage must be paid and endless time devoted. The most valuable of all resources is readily expended upon such empty, unsatisfying deities. What the quest for success does not devour, the lust for pleasure is lurking in the shadows to consume. Nothing is left but the often drug-induced lapse into oblivion that masquerades as sleep.

Understanding the table as an altar elevates mealtime from the mundane to the sublime. The table is not just a food-distribution device. It is a sacred place, a spiritual object. What is done there, including the consumption of food, is to be done with reverence and honor to God, the supreme provider. Even eating itself becomes a spiritual exercise, done with the expectation that when one has eaten and is full, he is then to praise the Lord for the bounty of his provision. As a matter of fact, giving thanks to God after the meal was God's very first worship instruction to Israel. The first liturgical exercise to be employed by the Israelites was to be a prayer of blessing and thanksgiving to God for the fact that he had provided food for them.[5] The God who is blessed at the beginning of the meal as the Sovereign who brings forth bread from the earth is again blessed at the end of the meal as the giver of both a good land and the food that it produces.

This most ancient of worship formulae in the Jewish community is called the *Birkath haMazon*. It first features a blessing of praise to God for being the one who feeds the entire world. It then continues with thanksgiving to God for providing a good and fruitful land with which he constantly sustains his children at every hour. It finally concludes with a prayer for God to have mercy upon his people Israel and upon Jerusalem and petitions God to continue to feed, nourish, sustain, support, and relieve his people.

By beginning and concluding every meal with prayers and blessing of thanksgiving, a Christian family can both give the praise to God that he deserves as the sustainer of life and, at the same time, elevate the entire family meal time to the level of sanctity and blessing that it should have. By recognizing that the table is a family altar and that everything that transpires around it is "holy unto the Lord," the family strengthens itself by strengthening each member of the family in the bonds of familial love and in the knowledge that God is the center of the family and its every activity.

[1] Malachi 1:7, 12.
[2] 1 Corinthians 10:21.
[3] Wendy Mogel, *The Blessing of a Skinned Knee: Using Jewish Teachings to Raise Self-Reliant Children* (New York: Simon & Schuster, 2001), p. 35.
[4] Deuteronomy 8:3; Matthew 4:4; Luke 4:4.
[5] Deuteronomy 8:10.

Chapter 7

A House of Meeting

A PLACE FOR FELLOWSHIP

The family temple is first of all a place of meeting. Just as Israel's wilderness sanctuary was called the tent of meeting, so the family table must become a place of fellowship for the entire family. The home must be a small version of the synagogal *Beth Knesset*, a place for secure and affirming interpersonal relationship as well as for spiritual fellowship with family and friends and with God.

The modern family spends far too little time in interpersonal interaction in the home. The hustle and bustle of modern life places so much individual time demands upon father, mother, and children that there is often no time left for corporate family interaction. Time is gobbled up by life's "important" activities, leaving the family-fellowship plate empty and the family relationship cupboard bare. The home has become more of a depot than a dwelling. Like Grand Central Station, different family members come chugging in on different tracks at different times and then head off in another direction with little more than a nod or a grunt to one another. Everyone is too busy for what really matters in life.

Then society laments the condition of its youth. Parents are clueless. Even the church seems helpless. Why are children murdering children? Why are young minds fried on drugs? Why are young people exploiting one another in virtually anonymous sexual trysts which are so void of any semblance of love that that they are almost mechanistically described by kids as "hooking up." Why do young people throw themselves into momentary exchanges of bodily fluids are little more than vehicles for sexually transmitted diseases, unwanted pregnancies, and, worse yet, abortion on demand?

There are two reasons. First, many parents have no interest in their children whatsoever. Like stallions standing at stud, some men sire children without even remotely considering the responsibility of fatherhood. Women who allow themselves to be victimized by these self-absorbed and self-consumed narcissists are faced with the dilemma of choosing abortion or bring a fetus to term. Whatever the choice, the cycle of abuse continues. The fatherless household, except for the grace of a loving mother— or more often than not, a grandmother—becomes a breeding ground for addiction, abuse, violence, and crime.

Second, there are the parents who have bought into the postmodern idea that children are their equals, that they should never be disciplined, and that they exist so that parents can dote on their every whim. "We don't understand," parents moan to themselves and to others, "we've given them everything." And that is precisely the problem: they have given their children every *thing*. The answer is so simple that it is too simple: too many modern parents give their children everything except time. Statistics say that the average American father currently spends all of two minutes a day with his children![1] What more could society expect from a pampered, narcissistic generation raised by parents who jump at their every command, always giving them more and more things but never setting the boundaries and restraints that provide genuine security and "love."

Then, generations have been reared under the specter of postmodernism's *nihilism*. Everything is nothing. Sated feelings and passions demand something even more exciting to sustain the existential moment. One drug leads to another and to another until brains are driven to mindlessness. One sexual adventure leads to another and to another until the most vile and violent must be experienced in order to satisfy the demons lurking in the human soul. No matter how much one gets, it is never enough. There are no boundaries because no one has the right to set any. Wants become rights, and rights demand fulfillment by whatever means.

Children have been educated by government school systems to believe that the only thing that matters is what they want. The ideas of their parents have been caricatured as religious "child abuse." Any parental discipline is cause for civil investigation. The state knows what it wants, and what it wants is an utterly godless society where there are no absolutes and children are raised, not reared. Entertainment and media moguls have led generations of children down the path of hedonism so that most are utterly lacking in social etiquette and basic human decency. Where God and biblical morality and ethics were once taught in school systems, now atheism, immorality, and situational ethics are trumpeted by godless professors, and vulnerable children are brainwashed.

Human nature demands social interaction. The human species is a gregarious sort. Young people will meet and greet, and they will go much further when they have no boundaries, no limitations. When the people they interrelate with are atheists or agnostics and narcissists, they will be influenced by the ideas and actions of those to mimic their lifestyles, and they will drift off into the netherworld of sin and debauchery, addiction and abuse. If, on the other hand, they are exposed to a continuing social relationship with godly parents and the influence of a larger godly community, they will mimic the lifestyles of their family and community leaders and maintain their values.

MAKING TIME FOR GODLY FELLOWSHIP

"Godly fellowship or community stands in stark contrast to what the world offers. . . . And its terrain has plenty of room for as many spiritual settlers as want to come—and who are willing to abide by Kingdom civics,"[2] says Andrew Arroyo. And, as Gilbert Beers notes, "We ignore godly fellowship at great peril, for God rewards godly fellowship with great blessing."[3] Indeed, "we often experience God more fully when we live in open relationship with each other."[4] There is no substitute for fellowship in which humans and God join in community in the *koinonia* (sharing) of the Spirit.

Each family, therefore, needs a specified time and a designated place for set-apart fellowship and interaction on two levels: the social and the spiritual. Time is needed to talk about the events of life and to listen to one another's needs and concerns. Just like God's children need to meet with their heavenly Father, family members need to meet regularly with one another. Children need quality time on a purely social level with their parents. Other times can be set apart for instruction and worship exercises. All of life, however, is not wrapped up in these important functions. Time must be made for conversation and interaction so that children can feel secure and can develop the social skills needed for successful lives.

Meeting around the table in the total absence of entertainment devices and media materials is a vital part of the family temple. Turn off the television. Stop the video games. Power down the smart phones: stop the texting and Internet browsing. Close Facebook. And, for God's sake, remove the ear buds, and turn off the music devices. Set aside the reading material (if any is left in the electronic era), and insist on time for communication.

Ah, there's a novel idea: teach children how to communicate with each other—and don't try to do it with texting on a "smart" phone. Spend quality time wherein the entire family can speak to one another with respect and affirmation. When social interaction occurs around a table that the entire family understands to be an altar, it will inevitably be wholesome and will reflect honor, mutuality, and respect.

Making your home a House of Fellowship also means making time for spiritual interrelationship with all the members of your family. While social interaction is important and is often woefully lacking in many Christian households, spiritual fellowship is even more vital. Children need to learn the blessing that communion in the home with family members as brothers and sisters in the body of the Messiah can provide. The home permits a level of intimacy and accountability that the church often lacks, especially in those communities where performance-based Christian experience dominates and where anonymity and lack of accountability result.

Discussing the spiritual aspects of human relationships among family members can provide greater understanding of feeling and emotions and give them context within the parameters for human relationships that are established by God's Word. Sitting around the family altar, parents and children can feel safe in expressing their feelings and needs. Their thoughts can be springboards for discussion of how the ways and will of God can be fulfilled in their lives.

The altar in the family *Beth Knesset* should be a place where the only question that is a stupid question is the one that is not asked. Children are naturally curious, and they can ask virtually unanswerable questions; however, just the asking in the safe and loving environment of the family temple can be just as important as getting an answer—or no answer. Expanding thoughts can explore various possibilities. Seemingly polarized, conflicting concepts can be held in dynamic tension when parents live patient, faith-based lives.

Godly fellowship in the home should not always be somber and morose. Indeed, laughter is as much a part of God's design for human beings as pensive reflection. "Godly fellowship enhances the life of the true worshipper," says Ava Baird. "A good time of laughter and Godly humor is enriching to the body, soul and spirit. Take some time out to have a good laugh; this gives balance to the life of the worshipper."[5] The family *Beth Knesset* can be a place for reflection, communication, sharing of pain and sorrow, and enjoyment of humor and laughter. This is the mix of human life and emotions, and the family temple is the place for all of these experiences to be shared to their fullest. If your House of Fellowship is always gloomy and ominous with a heavy spirit of glum, pseudo-pious religiosity, none of the family members, particularly children, will look forward to it. Make your *Beth Kenesset* a happy place, a time for children to look forward to sharing time with God and family in a real, honest-to-goodness enjoyable experience where they can feel at home and not in some strange, sad environment.

Above all, sanctify ("set apart") time in your House of Fellowship for God and your family. Don't allow societal pressures force you into such a hyperactive lifestyle that the most important people in your life are crowded out. Have a pre-scheduled time of meeting, and do it on a regular basis, at least weekly. You will be amazed to discover what God can and will do through you and your family in the sanctity of your family temple.

[1] George Howe Colt, *The Enigma of Suicide* (New York: Simon & Schuster, 1991), p. 53.
[2] Andrew Arroyo, *Seeds of Maturity for Personal and Communal Fruitfulness* (Longwood, FL: Xulon Press, 2003), p. 154.
[3] V. Gilbert Beers and Ronald A. Beers, eds., *TouchPoints Bible Promises: God's Answers for Your Daily Needs* (Carol Stream, IL: Tyndale House Publishers, 2000), p. 97.
[4] Beers and Beers, p. 97.
[5] Ava Patricia Baird, *True Worshippers* (Victoria, BC: Trafford Publishing, 2007), p. 22.

Chapter 8

A House of Study

A PLACE FOR LEARNING

The table as an altar is also designed to be a small version of the synagogal *Beth Midrash*, a place for study. Herein is manifest another profound Jewish concept that has been largely lost to the Christian understanding—the fact that study is worship. Most Christians conceive of worship as something that is done in church with one's eyes closed. Study and learning are recognized as necessary for a successful life; however, they are almost never considered to be worship.

When the biblical concept of worship is examined, however, it is clear that it entails far more than enraptured euphoria or the emotion of an existential moment. The Hebrew word for worship is שָׁחָה (*shachah*), which means to "prostrate oneself" (as in the presence of the Deity). This word clearly pictures the ultimate submission that true worship requires. The Greek word for worship, προσκυνέω (*proskuneo*), is even more graphic, implying a level of submission to God that is parallel with that of a dog licking its master's hand. True worship is not a struggle to achieve the warm-fuzzies. It is prostration—lying flat on the ground before God. Every fiber of one's being is submitted to God and his instructions. One may not be required to be prostrated literally and physically; however, the attitude of the heart must be one of total submission to God if true worship is manifest.

Study, therefore, is a high form of worship, for it is study of the Word of God, with a view toward doing the Word, which is the very essence of submission to God. The idea of acquiring knowledge of God's Word with no commitment to doing it is foreign to Judaism. While knowledge of the Word of God for its own sake is a paramount virtue in Judaism,[1] learning without action is unthinkable.[2] The emphasis among the Jewish people is always on the doing. Jews have an insatiable desire to know God's Word, but they also have an unquenchable passion to fulfill it. Greeks study only to know; Jews study in order to revere![3] Christians study for creed; Jews study for deed. Christians study to believe; Jews study to do. And, in doing so, Jews are closer to the biblical formula than many Christians.

When confronted with the fire on Mount Sinai and the powerful words of God's Law thundering in their ears, the Israelites did not say, "All that you say, we will believe." They affirmed, "All that you say, we will do."[4] Jesus, the Jew, affirmed this principle: "Let your light so shine before men that they may see your *good works* and glorify your Father in heaven."[5] Again, the Savior did not say, "Let your light shine before men that they may see your *faith*." While faith is utterly vital, "faith without works is dead."[6] Status before God (righteousness) is gained and maintained solely by faith, for it is only by grace through faith that people are saved.[7] The eternal principle that no one has ever been nor can be saved or have status before God by either works or knowledge is both a Jewish and a Christian insight. At the same time, it is an eternal biblical principle that faith for salvation and acceptance before God automatically produces good works of obedience to God's Word.[8]

The foundational confession of Jewish faith, the *Shema*

("Hear, O Israel, the LORD our God, the LORD is one") rests on its first word, *hear*, a word that means "to hear and do.[9] Israel's initial response to God's thundering discourse from Sinai was, "All that you have said, we will do, and we will hear [intelligently]."[10] In a supra-logical formula, Israel confessed that they would do God's Word first and then understand (hear) it. More often than not, God's instructions are ineffable. They seem illogical to the rational human mind (which "hates God"[11]). In order to understand them, one must first do them. This, in turn, requires the supreme submission to God by studying in order to do before understanding comes. This is why it is vital for everyone to do God's instructions before he or she undertakes the work of teaching them to others. The wisdom of doing before teaching is set forth very clearly in the approach that Ezra took to God's Word: "Ezra had prepared his heart to study the law of the LORD and to do it, and to teach in Israel statutes and judgments."[12] This is especially true in the home, for children will always do what their parents do, not just what they say or what they tell them to do. The old adage, "Do as I say, not as I do," simply never works. Children will do what they see their parents do.

Study in the Jewish home, then, is a high form of worship. It is another of the worship exercises that transpire around the family altar, the table. The bread from the earth is consumed as an exercise that leads immediately into the consumption of the bread from heaven, the living Word of God. Every Christian home would profit from this example so that family mealtime will feature both earthly and heavenly food, nourishing both the outer and the inner man. When this approach is taken, bread from the earth (*lechem min ha-aretz*) becomes bread from heaven (*lechem min ha-shamayim*), the manna of ancient times that was bread from God's table.[13]

One profound, residual benefit of consuming the Word of

God is the fact that it strengthens covenantal relationships. The spiritual bonds that cement familial relations are ever strengthened by partaking of God's Word. Human relationships are polished to pristine purity by mutual commitment to God's revealed will. Unity that is just as much needed in both the domestic scene as it is in the ecclesiastical realm is fostered when individuals come to the full knowledge of God's Son, the person of his Word.[14] Just as the sanctifying truth of God's Word unites disciples of Christ in a unity that is parallel with the unity of the Heavenly Father and the divine Son,[15] so the living Word cements the bonds of family solidarity. Sharing God's Word around the family altar puts everything that is needed on the table to build strong godly character in all family members. It demonstrates the fact that God's instructions apply to all. Parents are responsible, therefore, to speak God's Word to their children and then to model that divine insight before their children so that the children then can imitate their parents in lives of faith and purity.

Study in Hebraic tradition is not, however, limited to the study of God's Word. As a matter of fact, all study is considered worship because there is no dichotomy between "spiritual" knowledge and "secular" knowledge in Hebraic thought. The spirit that is in human beings is given "understanding" by the "breath of the Almighty."[16] All educational pursuits, therefore, should be considered to be "spiritual" exercises. The home, consequently, should be the center for education in every aspect of life. This is why parents should equip their children with resources and why every home should have a library as a part of the *Beth Midrash* function of its family temple. Wise parents follow the advice of Solomon: "Train up a child in the way he should go."[17] The emphasis in this passage on training in the way the child should go is clear from the literal translation of the passage. The word translated "train" is חָנַךְ (*hanak*), the word from which the

Hebrew word *ḥanukkah* ("dedication") is derived. The root of this word means to "initiate" or "to narrow." *Hanak* also means "to teach" or "to educate." Then, the word translated "way" is דֶּרֶךְ (*derek*), a word that is cognate with the word *darak* which means "to bend" as in the bending a bow.[18] Finally, the word interpreted to mean "he should go" is פֶּה (*peh*) which means "mouth" or "opening." With this in mind, Proverbs 22:6 can be translated, "Start a child at the opening of his path," or "Train a child in the direction of his bent."

Second, the grammar of the text makes another cardinal point clear. The entire sentence is written in the singular, not the plural: it says, "Train a child," not "Train children." This is very important, for it makes it clear that Scripture does not promote a "one-size-fits-all" approach to educating children. Each child's individuality is to be respected, and the training that parents are responsible for giving to their children is to be tailored first and foremost to the child.

Marvin Wilson notes a great truth when he says, "There is a great difference between the training of a child according to the *child's* way (i.e., encouraging him to start on the road that is right for him), and training him according to the way chosen, prescribed, and imposed by the parents. The former is in keeping with the child's unique God-given bent, disposition, talents, and gifts. It is considerate of the uniqueness of the child; it does not treat all developing personalities the same." In short, Wilson concludes, "The instruction of youth, the education of youth, ought to be conformed to the nature of youth."[19]

This interpretation of Proverbs 22:6 is the foundation of the Hebraic understanding that parents have a two-fold responsibility: 1) teaching their children the precepts of the eternal Word of God and 2) teaching their children a means of livelihood that is in accord with the child's talents and inclinations. In Jewish tradition, then, wise parents are careful to respect their

children's individuality by observing them from infancy to discern what gift or inclination the child innately has. Then, they do
everything in their power to facilitate the development of that
bent, "his way," by providing educational opportunities that move
the child along the path that is right for the child.

Far too often, however, parents who were unable to realize
their childhood or adult dreams wish to impose those on their
children, forcing children into careers for which they are not
inclined or gifted. Children are biological descendants of their
parents, not clones of their parents. To force a child to be and
do what the parent envisions is to engage in selfishness which
can only lead to disappointment for the child and the parent.

Wise parents will be diligent to observe their children from
infancy to see where the child's interests lie. This requires continuing interest in the child's activities, thoughts, feelings, and
emotions. Sometimes subtly, sometimes overtly, signs of the
inclination and gift that God has implanted in the child will
emerge. With such observation and a commitment to the biblical premise of training a child in the way he should go, parents
can start the child on his path, the path that will bring self-worth
and self-fulfillment to the child that will continue and grow over
a lifetime.

The family temple as a *Beth Midrash*, then, is a powerful
dynamic, one that is woefully neglected in so many Christian
homes. Far too often, the education of Christian children is left
entirely to public educational systems that are dominated by
postmodernism and humanism that are inimical to the core values
of Christian faith. It is time that Christian parents assume their
responsibility to teach their own children the ways of the Lord
and to provide for them educational opportunities that are not
controlled forms of brainwashing at the hands of militant secularist systems. The only way that solid biblical values can be
propelled into a constantly changing future is for parents to take

charge, do their God-given job, and make their home a house of God, a true house of study, a Christian *Beth Midrash*. The ominous threat that postmodernism, New Age philosophy, and neopaganism poses not only to the continued existence of Christianity but also to the very survival of civilization can only be met with a focus on the family temple and especially on its functions as a *Beth Midrash*. Christians must learn the lesson from the Jewish people that has ensured the survival of both Jews and Judaism through centuries of unrelenting, systematic abuse, violence, and mayhem. Marvin Wilson succinctly points out the truth that is the answer to the dilemma of Christianity in the postmodern era when he speaks of the reason for the continuing survival of Judaism: "Because of the way it is structured, Judaism will always survive in the home. . . . As a layperson, the parent is responsible to be familiar with the teachings of Judaism in order to serve as teacher within the sanctuary of the home."[20]

[1] Shmuley Boteach, *Judaism for Everyone: Renewing Your Life Through the Vibrant Lessons of the Jewish Faith* (New York: Basic Books, 2002), p. xxv.

[2] Abraham Joshua Heschel, *God in Search of Man: Philosophy of Judaism* (New York: Farrar, Straus, and Cudahy, 1955), pp. 2-3, 43-53, 73-79.

[3] Judith R. Baskin, *The Cambridge Dictionary of Judaism and Jewish Culture* (Cambridge: Cambridge University Press, 2011), p. 145.

[4] Exodus 19:8; 24:3.

[5] Matthew 5:16.

[6] James 2:17-20.

[7] Ephesians 2:8.

[8] John 15:10; 1 John 2:3; James 2:22.

[9] Deuteronomy 6:4.

[10] Exodus 24:7.

[11] Romans 8:7.

[12] Ezra 7:10.

[13] John 6:31-32.

[14] Ephesians 4:13.

[15] John 17:17-21.

[16] Job 33:4.

[17] Proverbs 22:6.

[18] Psalm 11:2; 64:3; Jeremiah 46:9.

[19] Marvin R. Wilson, *Our Father Abraham: Jewish Roots of the Christian Faith* (Grand Rapids, MI: Wm. B. Eerdmans Publishing Co., 1989), pp. 293, 294.

[20] Wilson, p. 216.

Chapter 9

A House of Prayer

A PLACE FOR FAMILY PRAYER AND WORSHIP

The family temple is also designed to be a miniature version of the synagogal *Beth Tefillah* (House of Prayer). The family table is also an altar that serves as a center for family prayer and worship. The ancient temple in Israel was called a "house of prayer for all people."[1] It was only natural, therefore, that the synagogue also came to be called a *Beth Tefillah*. Similarly, the prayer and worship activities of the ancient family also made the home a house of prayer.

The fact that "House of Prayer" was one of the three terms used to describe the temple and the synagogue underscores the importance of prayer in the lives of believers. Indeed, all of the worship activities in which believers engage can be lumped together under the heading of prayer, for prayer is conversation with God. Not merely meditation or contemplation, it is the outpouring of the heart addressed directly to the Eternal. It is not, however, merely one-way communication, for in prayer God speaks to those who seek him. Samuel Ballentine maintains that in the tradition of the Hebrew Scriptures, "prayer is a primary means of communication which binds God and people into intimate and reciprocal relationship."[2] It can also be "manifest in a variety of nonspeech approaches to God, e.g., song, sacrifice, dance, any one of which deserves its own place in the study of prayer."[3] Prayer, then, is an overarching term that encompasses every outpouring of the human heart toward God, including postures of the body and other forms of nonverbal communication.

PRAYER

The term *Beth Tefillah* was used to describe the temple and the synagogue because prayer was the predominant activity that took place in God's house. The Israelites believed that God both heard and answered prayer. They also believed that he dwelled among his people. Solomon exclaimed during his prayer of dedication to the temple he had built, "Will God indeed dwell on earth? behold, the heaven and heaven of heavens cannot contain you, how much less this house which I have built?" Then, in faith, he continued to pray, "When your people . . . turn to you and confess your name and pray . . . whatever prayer or supplication is made by any man or by all your people Israel, each . . . spreading his hands toward this house; then hear in heaven your dwelling place, and forgive and act and render to each according to all his ways."[4]

Solomon's prayer for Israel was then made universal by his inclusion of all people: "Also concerning the foreigner who is not of your people Israel . . . when he comes and prays toward this house, hear in heaven your dwelling place, and do according to all for which the foreigner calls to you, in order that all the peoples of the earth may know your name."[5] This is why the temple was called a "house of prayer for all people." Prayer, then, is designed to be a central part of each family temple, no matter where in the world it may be, whether a Jewish or a Gentile home.

The centrality of prayer is underscored in the Jewish community by the focus on corporate prayers in the synagogue. This liturgical exercise is facilitated by *Siddurim* (prayer books) which

outline the standard forms and orders of prayers. This practice
dates to before the time of Jesus. Significant Jewish prayers that
predate the time of Jesus include the *Shema*, the *Amidah*, and the
Kaddish prayers. The *Shema* is foundational to all Jewish faith and
was declared by Jesus to be the "first" and "greatest" commandment, so it was certainly prayed by Jesus and the apostles.[6] The
Amidah, which is called "The Prayer" in Judaism, dates to the
fifth century BC and was certainly used during the time of Jesus.
It is also very likely that the *Kaddish* was prayed by the disciples
because it dates to the first century BC.[7]

The likelihood that Jesus and the disciples did, indeed, pray
the collective prayers of Judaism in their customary worship in
the synagogues[8] is confirmed by the description of the lifestyles
of the earliest Jewish Christian believers in Acts 2:42 where
Luke noted that the disciples "devoted themselves to the apostles'
teaching and to fellowship, to the breaking of bread and to
prayer." The meaning of this statement in relationship to
"prayers" becomes clear from the Greek text which says that
they were devoted to ταῖς προσευχαῖς—*tais proseuchais*, "*the*
prayers." Virtually all translations and interpretations say that
the disciples were devoted to prayer; however, the text uses the
definite article and uses the plural *prayers*.[9]

Interestingly enough, it was the disciples who asked Jesus
to "teach us to pray," whereupon he gave them the immortal
words of what has come to be called the Lord's Prayer.[10] This
prayer, however, was not an innovation, for it simply condensed
in précis form the words of the synagogue prayers that predated
the time of Jesus. There was no effort on the part either of Jesus
or of the disciples to break from the Jewish prayer tradition
wherein they had been reared. Doubtless, the "Lord's Prayer"
would have been a significant part of the disciples' prayer lives
after the ascension of Jesus; however, they obviously continued
in "*the* prayers" of their ancient faith, biblical Judaism.

This tradition was a part of the concept of praying the Word of God. Because there are many profound prayers throughout the pages of the Bible, it is obvious that they are efforts by God-breathed Scripture[11] to inculcate the principles of prayer into the lives of believers. Indeed, it is impossible to "ask amiss"[12] if one is praying the Word of God. God's Word simply works. When believers pray what God's Word said, they have every reason to expect the outcome of prayer that God promises.[13] Whether prayer is liturgical or spontaneous, it is certainly a central part of the life of the believer. As James said, "The effective prayer of a righteous person can accomplish much."[14]

When considering this aspect of the family temple, one immediately recognizes that a motto from a previous generation still says it all today: "The family that prays together stays together."[15] This saying has never been more clearly manifest than in the traditional Jewish home, where prayers and blessings have been continually spoken around the table, prayers that have solidified the Jewish family and supported its resolve to stand for God's truth even in the most insidious and violent attacks against the Jewish faith and the Jewish people themselves. The Jewish family and community has survived and maintained its identity and its faith because Jewish families have prayed and worshipped together around the family altar.

The home, then, is a center for spiritual development as well as for social and educational development, and the table is an altar from which prayer and worship should be daily offered. No matter how large or small, how formal or simple, the table is the family altar when it is dedicated to God and his service. At the family table, parents can engage in prayer, Bible reading, study, song, and in acts of charity and kindness. Participating in each of these worship exercises impresses upon both parents and children the importance of standing in solidarity with one another in the presence of God by speaking and hearing God's

Word and invoking God's blessing upon the family unit and upon each of its members. Virtually all of the worship exercises that believers experience in corporate, congregational devotion can be enjoyed in the sanctity of the family temple. In the same way that leaders of congregations lead their assemblies in worship, parents, as priests in their homes, can lead their families in praise, worship, song, Bible reading, and prayer.

READING THE WORD OF GOD

Reading the Holy Scriptures aloud is a significant part of the worship experience of the family temple, just as it is in the corporate assemblies of the Christian community. In Roman Catholic tradition, the Word and the sacrament were virtually inseparable.[16] For the Anglican Church, the communion service had three major sections, the introductory material, the "liturgy of the Word," and the "liturgy of the Upper Room."[17] John Calvin and Martin Luther maintained that the truly distinctive marks of the church were the Word and the sacraments, which they viewed as limited communion and baptism.[18] Calvin, however, elevated the Word to a status of greater importance than communion with his declaration, "Without the Word, the sacrament is but a dumb show. The Word must go before."[19] Both Luther and Calvin were wrestling with the historical Catholic teaching regarding sacramentalism which maintained that the sacraments were necessary for salvation and that they were efficacious regardless as to the condition of heart of either the celebrant or the communicant.[20]

From a purely biblical perspective, stripped of historical church tradition, the Word and the sacrament are the central manifestations of Christian corporate worship. This is true also in the context of worship in the family temple, the home. The priority of the Word as the source and foundation of the sacrament, however, is clearly established in Scripture. Without the authority of the Word, neither communion nor baptism has any foundation or efficacy.

The importance of study and reading of the Word of God in the home cannot, therefore, be overemphasized. It is the Word of God enunciated in the Gospel of Jesus Christ that is the power of God unto salvation,[21] for "faith comes by hearing, and hearing by the word of God."[22] As the Psalmist confessed: "I have hidden your word in my heart that I might not sin against you."[23] The wise person is the one who meditates on God's Word day and night.[24] And this "meditation" is not merely a mental exercise. In the Hebrew understanding of the word הָגָה—hagah ("meditate") means to verbalize the words of Scripture over and over again until they have become a part of the individual or the community. The image is that of a ruminating cow, chewing the food, swallowing, regurgitating, chewing again, and swallowing again until the food is fully digested. This is a part of the image of ingesting the Word of God that was employed to describe the experience of both Ezekiel and John, who "ate the scroll"[25] so that the Word became a part of the very fiber of their beings.

The family temple is a perfect place for the Word of God to be read and discussed. Parents can easily lead this essential part of worship. Children can also read Bible verses or texts. Then, the texts can be explained and discussed sometimes in ways that are not possible in the context of traditional public worship exercises. This kind of interactive learning was part and parcel of the worship experience of the primitive Hebrew community, the Israelites, and the earliest Christian church, for the public assemblies were essentially domestic affairs where extended families gathered to fulfill the divine commandments for assembling together, and in the context of those assemblies read and discussed the Scriptures among themselves.

The reading of the Word of God should be the foremost

and leading experience in the "House of Prayer" function of the family mini-temple. It only takes a few minutes to read a verse or a portion of Scripture, and since there are 31,173 verses in the Bible, the choices are unlimited. You will never run out of Scripture to read. If you read one verse a day, it would take 85 years to read all the Bible! Remember that every time you read Scripture, you and your family are hearing God's Word, and God's Word works.

If you wonder what to read and when to read it, many lectionaries (books or lists of Scripture readings appointed for Christian or Jewish worship on a given day) are available, including those on the Internet. You may wish to read the Torah portion (the *parashah* or section of the Pentateuch that has been prescribed for each week by the sages of Israel). This is what Jesus did in his time. You may also wish to employ one of many Christian lectionaries. You can also devise your own outline for reading the Word. Whatever choice you make as to system, be sure that you make yourself and your family avid readers of the Word of God. May it be said of your children as it was said of Timothy: "From a child you have known the holy scriptures, which are able to make you wise unto salvation through faith which is in Christ Jesus."[26] Remember also Paul's explanation: "All scripture is inspired by God and profitable for teaching, for reproof, for correction, for training in righteousness: so that the person dedicated to God may be capable and equipped for every good work."[27] It is only through dedication to the reading of Holy Scripture that parents and children can be undergirded with the solid foundation of God's Word.

COMMUNION

Christianity's most central recurring sacrament is holy communion, the ceremony in which Jesus instructed his disciples to engage themselves in remembrance of his death.[28] While much discussion has been undertaken to determine how, when, where, by whom, and how frequently communion can or should be celebrated, the truth is that this worship experience is fundamental to Christian faith because it fulfills the specific commandment of Jesus. It is certain that this worship experience continued in the earliest church because Paul commanded the church to celebrate communion and outlined the order for its observance: "For I received from the Lord that which I also delivered to you, that the Lord Jesus in the night in which he was betrayed took bread; and when he had given thanks, he broke it and said, 'This is my body, which is for you; do this in remembrance of me.' In the same way he took the cup also after supper, saying, 'This cup is the new covenant in my blood; do this, as often as you drink it, in remembrance of me.' For as often as you eat this bread and drink the cup, you proclaim the Lord's death until he comes."[29]

When Paul gave this instruction, he was advising the believers in Corinth as to how they should observe communion in corporate worship; however, there is no Scriptural restriction on the observance of communion in other settings as well. When the ancient Jewish precursors of communion are considered, it becomes obvious that communion can be celebrated in the context of family worship, for both of those ancient Jewish celebrations were first and foremost family events. Though the organized church has carefully restricted communion observance to that which is carried out by the professional clergy, it is clear that no such restrictions were placed upon believers in the earliest days of original Christianity.

The most prominent antecedent of communion—and, indeed, its very foundation—was Passover, the ceremony that was first celebrated in individual Israelite homes where extended family and friends were invited into the family temple to eat of the Paschal lamb, the *matzah*, and the bitter herbs that God

commanded the Israelites to share.[30] Even strangers were invited
into the Jewish homes to share the Passover.[31] Jesus himself
continued the tradition that he had received from his Jewish
family by celebrating the Passover on the last night of his life on
earth, the night of his betrayal.[32] It was then that he used the
unleavened bread and the wine that were central elements of the
traditional Passover observance and instituted holy communion
by pouring new meaning into the ancient ritual and command-
ing his disciples to celebrate Passover thereafter not only to
memorialize their deliverance from Egyptian bondage, but also
to remember his death and the deliverance from sin that his
blood provided for them.[33] Communion, therefore, was instituted on the night of a Passover that was being observed in a
family setting, the extended family of Jesus.[34]

Communion is also anchored historically and practically in
the weekly *Shabbat* meal, which is introduced in Jewish homes by
blessings to God for the provision of bread and wine. This
celebration of praise to God with bread and wine is at least as
ancient as the time of Abraham and Melchizedek, for when the
king-priest of Salem received tithes from the patriarch of faith
and blessed him, he brought forth bread and wine.[35] The blessings that Jesus himself spoke over the bread and wine were the
same benedictions that his ancestors had recited as they celebrated *Shabbat* and the Passover with their families.[36] As Jesus
instituted a new Passover order, the Scriptures specifically say
that he "blessed" God when he introduced the bread[37] and "gave
thanks" when he introduced the wine.[38]

Jesus very likely, therefore, spoke these same time-honored
words that the Jewish people use when they bless God for the
bread and the wine in their Passover and Sabbath family worship
exercises: "*Barukh attah Adonai, Elohenu, Melekh ha-olam, ha-motzi
lechem min ha-aretz . . . Barukh attah Adonai, Elohenu, Melekh ha-
olam, borey pri ha-gafen*" ("Blessed are you, O Lord our God, King

of the universe, who brings forth bread from the earth . . . Blessed are you, O Lord our God, King of the universe, who creates the fruit of the vine.").[39] These blessings were given on both Passover and *Shabbat* first in the context of family and then in the context of corporate worship.

Communion, then, was originally celebrated in both families and extended family communities. When the family celebrates communion, there was no need for a priest or minister to be present to bless the bread and the fruit of the vine, for neither needs blessing. Jesus himself did not bless the bread or the wine because neither needed blessed since neither required blessing in order to be "holy." This was in keeping with the biblical and Jewish understanding that everything that God created was good, not evil.[40] Both elements employed in communion, therefore, are inherently good, as they have been from the time of creation. These elements are not profane and do not, therefore, need to be blessed in order to make them "holy." Rather than blessing things, the family priest is qualified to bless (praise) the Lord and give thanks to him just as Jesus did. Then, each participant can discern in the bread and in the wine the body and blood of Jesus as he eats the bread and drinks the wine.[41] The bread and wine of communion can be shared in the family setting at any time, including those times when food would normally be consumed in the family temple.

What better way is there to teach children that Jesus is the bread of life and that his blood cleanses from all sin than to "do this in remembrance of [him]" in the intimacy and security of the home? Having so received the communion of the living Christ in their family temple, families are prepared to celebrate and receive the larger community of believers into the continually expanding family circle of the church that is in communion with one another and with the living Lord. Communion in the corporate worship setting merely confirms and strengthens the communion that is received in the family temple.

MUSIC, SONG, AND DANCE

Song, in particular, is something that is often missing in Christian homes. Here a great lesson can also be learned from the Jewish people for whom *zimrot* ("songs") are an integral part of family worship. HaLevi and Frankel note a profound truth when they say that "joyous song is perhaps one of the greatest forms of prayer."[42] They also underscore the words of Rabbi Aaron of Karlin who said, "Jews express their faith most fully and most joyfully when they sing out unreservedly."[43] Song elevates the human spirit into God's presence while at the same time inculcating eternal truths in a way in which they are remembered throughout the lifetime of each family member.

This is why even the *berachot* for the bread and wine are often sung and why the husband's blessing for his wife (Proverbs 31) is often sung as well. There is something about putting he words of Holy Scripture and biblical blessings to song that elevates the meaning and experience. Song also makes the words far more memorable, especially for children.

Dance also has long been a feature of the worship experience of the Hebrew and Jewish peoples. One only need to turn to the experiences and words of King David to see the importance and value of dance to the dynamics of worshipping God. Who could forget the great exercise of praise when David "danced with all his might" in the presence of the returned and restored Ark of the Covenant.[44] Then, in Psalm 150, David penned these words of instruction and inspiration in the litany of praise options that can be employed in the worship of God: "Praise [the LORD] with the tambourine and dance" (v.4). According to David, God deserves to be praised as much in the dance as he does with trumpets (v.3), harps and lyres (v.3), stringed instruments and flutes (v.4), and cymbals (v.6). David began this litany of praise with these words: "Praise ye the LORD! Praise God in his sanctuary; praise him in his mighty expanse" (v.1), and he concluded it with this exhortation: "Let everything that has breath praise the LORD! Praise ye the LORD!" (v.6).

Then, to make sure that the Psalmist's reference to dance was not just an obscure, cryptic statement that could be ignored or explained away, God had the sacred author repeat the instruction unequivocally in Psalm 149:2: "Let Israel be glad in his Maker. Let the sons of Zion rejoice in their King. Let them praise his name with dancing." While virtually all Christians would agree that God can be praised with harps, stringed instruments, and flutes, some would argue that dance is inappropriate as a medium of worship. The instruction for dance in worship, however, is clearly a part of the "all Scripture" that is God-breathed and profitable for teaching in the Christian assembly (2 Timothy 3:16). Christians are, therefore, as free to express their love and worship of God in the dance as they are in song, Scripture reading, and prayer.

Rather than having the music and lyrics of secular—and often profane, if not downright obscene—songs pulsating and echoing through your home, why not institute the practice of hearing the songs of Zion and of the Christian community in your home and of singing them yourself with your family, especially your children. The beautiful words and inspiring music of various Jewish songs can also elevate your family worship experience to a new level of praise to God and inspiration to one another.

BLESSING

Blessing was an integral part of the worship experience of the ancient Hebrews, the primitive Jewish community, and the earliest Christians. Blessing God with forms of praise and benediction and blessing others was a part of the everyday life of these biblical peoples. Even the greeting that said, "Hello," and the parting salutation that said, "Goodbye," was a biblical blessing contained in one word: *Shalom* (peace). See the next chapter for a thorough discussion of the subject of blessing as it relates to the family temple. Suffice it to say at this point that blessing was a significant ongoing part of the *Beit Tefillah* experience that was carried out in biblical times both in the family temple and in the temple and synagogues of God's chosen people. The subject of blessing in the home is discussed in detail in Chapter 10.

Continuing Daily Prayer, Praise, and Worship

If the most sacred of Christian worship experiences can be shared in the context of the family temple as well as in the corporate sanctuary, virtually any other act of worship can also be celebrated in the context of the family. What the familial priesthood has administered in the mini-temple is expanded and magnified when the priest-leader of the congregation celebrates in the corporate community temple. Christians need to reconsider and restore what has been lost to the family and the home by the segregation of some, if not most of the actions of prayer, praise, and worship away from the home and the cloistering of such experiences in the sanctuaries of corporate worship facilities and experiences. It is time for the family temple to become a true house of prayer and worship that employs every dimension of biblical expressions of devotion to God and of fellowship with one another in an invigorating, ongoing, daily exercise in the sanctity of acts of devotion around the family altar.

[1] Isaiah 56:7; Mark 11:17.
[2] Samuel E. Balentine, "Prayer/Thanksgiving in the Old Testament," in *Mercer Dictionary of the Bible*, Watson E. Mills and Roger Aubery Bullard, eds. (Macon, GA: Mercer University Press, 1990), p. 706.
[3] Balentine, p. 706.
[4] 1 Kings 8:3, 38-39.
[5] 1 Kings 8:41-42.

[6] Matthew 22:38.

[7] Hugh Fogelman, *Christianity Uncovered: Viewed Through Open Eyes* (Bloomington, IN: AuthorHouse, 2012), p. 342.

[8] Matthew 13:54; Mark 1:21; 6:2; Luke 4:16; John 18:20.

[9] Craig Steiner, *Moving Forward by Looking Back: Embracing First-Century Practices in Youth* (Grand Rapids, MI: Zondervan Publishing House, 2009), p. 17. Steiner argues that the earliest believers "had common prayers that were written and then repeated verbally." The question that begs to be asked is, Why would the disciples have created their own written prayers when they already had formalized prayers that they and their ancestors had prayed in the synagogues for perhaps centuries?

[10] Luke 11:1-4.

[11] 2 Timothy 3:16.

[12] James 4:3.

[13] Mark 11:24; 1 John 3:22.

[14] James 5:16.

[15] This slogan was composed by Al Scalpone, a professional commercial writer, for the purpose of promoting a Roman Catholic Family Rosary Crusade by Father Patrick Peyton in 1952. See George Latimer Apperson, *Dictionary of Proverbs* (Hertfordshire, UK: Wordsworth Editions Limited, 1993), p. 191.

[16] Anscar J. Chupungco, *Liturgical Inculturation: Sacraments, Religiosity, and Catechesis* (Collegeville, MN: The Liturgical Press, 1992), p. 83.

[17] Timothy Rosendale, *Liturgy and Literature in the Making of Protestant England* (Cambridge: Cambridge University Press, 2007), p. 211. Also D. E. W. Harrison, *Common Prayer* (Norwich, UK: Canterbury Press, 1946), pp. 67ff.

[18] G. W. Locher, *Sign of the Advent: A Study of Protestant Ecclesiology* (Fribourg: Academic Press, 2004), p. 88. Also Sandra Arenas, "Merely Quantifiable Realities? The 'Vestigia Ecclesiae' in the Thought of Calvin and its Twentieth-Century Reception" in Eddy Van Der Borgh and Gerald Mannion eds., *John Calvin's Ecclesiology: Ecumenical Perspectives* (New York: T&T Clark International, 2011), pp. 69-80.

[19] John Calvin, *Institutes of the Christian Religion,* IV.xvii.39. See Donald Macleod, *Presbyterian Worship: Its Meaning and Method* (Richmond, VA: John Knox Press, 1965), p. 62. Also, Howard G. Hageman, *Pulpit & Table: Some Chapters in the History of Worship in the Reformed Churches* (Richmond, VA: John Knox Press, 1962), p. 112, and Robert Letham, *The Lord's Supper: Eternal Word in Broken Bread* (Phillipsburg, NJ: P & R Publishing, 2011), p. 50.

[20] Stanley J. Grenz, *Theology for the Community of God* (Grand Rapids, MI: Wm. B. Eerdmans Publishing Co., p. 513. Grenz notes that in the Catholic view of the sacraments, "grace came without regard to the spiritual condition of either the participant or administrator (priest). So long as the recipient did not resist the working of God in the sacraments, when duly administered these acts infused grace by their very operation (*ex opere operato*).

[21] Romans 1:16.

[22] Romans 10:17.

[23] Psalm 119:11.

[24] Psalm 1:1-2.

[25] Ezekiel 2:9–3:1; Revelation 10:9.

[26] 2 Timothy 3:15.

[27] 2 Timothy 3:16-17, NASB, NET.

[28] Luke 22:19.

[29] 1 Corinthians 11:23-26.

[30] Numbers 9:11.

[31] Exodus 12:48.

[32] Matthew 26:26-27.

[33] Luke 22:19; 1 Corinthians 11:26.

[34] Mark 14:14-17.

[35] Genesis 14:18.

[36] Hans F. Bayer, *Jesus' Predictions of Vindication and Resurrection: The Provenance, Meaning, and Correlation of the Synoptic Predictions* (Tübingen: J.C.B. Mohr, 1986), pp. 38-39.

[37] Matthew 26:26.

[38] Mark 14:23.

[39] The text of Matthew 26:26 says that Jesus took the bread and blessed. Translations insert the word *it* after the word *blessed* because of the Christian tradition that food needs to be blessed and that elements that are used in sacred contexts need to be blessed because before they are blessed, they are profane. The texts of Matthew 26:27; Mark 14:26; and Luke 22:17 say that Jesus took the cup and "gave thanks." In all of these instances, the meaning of the texts is clear: Jesus blessed God for the provision of both the bread and the wine, and he did so in the tradition of the Jewish people that was employed in his time.

[40] Paul made this clear: "I am persuaded of the Lord Jesus that nothing is unclean of itself" (Romans 14:14). Anthony C. Thiselton says, "The Jewish table grace expressed *blessing God* for God's good gifts. . . . If we compare *m. Berakoth* 8:1-5 with *m. Peshaim* 10:2-7, whether the context is grace at meals or the blessing of God for the three cups at the Passover meal, 'saying the Benediction' uniformly means *blessing God for his gifts, not* 'blessing' the gifts." See Anthony C. Thieselton, *The First Epistle to the Corinthians: A Commentary on the Greek Text* (Grand Rapids, MI: Wm. B. Eerdmans Publishing Co., 2000), pp. 870-871. Also, Herbert Danby, *The Mishnah* (New York: Oxford University Press, 1933), pp. 8-9 and 150-151.

[41] 1 Corinthians 11:29.

[42] Baruch HaLevi and Ellen Frankel, *Revolution of Jewish Spirit: How to Revive Ruakh in Your Spiritual Life, Transform your Synagogue, and Inspire Your Jewish Community* (Woodstock, VT: Jewish Lights Publishing, 2012) p. 67.

[43] HaLevi and Frankel, p. 67.

[44] 2 Samuel 6:14.

Chapter 10

A Temple of Blessing

HAVING A BLESSED HOME

Viewing the home as more than a domicile where families eat, sleep, and watch television is the first step toward returning the home to its biblically Hebraic construct. In God's plan, the home has always been designed to be a temple, a place for the impartation of divine blessings that were originally created and bestowed in the context of the family. The home is a blessed place because it is designed by God to be a temple of blessing.

In the true spirit of divine blessing, anything that is blessed is blessed to be a blessing. God established this principle in his words to Abraham, "I will bless you . . . and you will be a blessing . . . in you all the families of the earth will be blessed."[1] God's blessing was always designed to be a blessing. It was for this reason that God blessed and set apart the Sabbath so that it could be a blessing to humanity. *Shabbat* is a channel for divine blessing both in the home and in the community. This is why the Jewish home is filled with the spirit of blessing throughout the Sabbath, which begins with a blessing and ends with a benediction. This blessing exercise that is employed by the Jewish family on the Sabbath is a great lesson for all believers. The same principles that bless Jewish families can also be employed in the context of the Christian family Sabbath, and they will result in the same blessing.

A significant part of God's original blessing for Abraham was that the patriarch's blessing was also to be transgenerational. This is clear from God's repetition to Abraham's son Isaac of precisely the same promise: "In you and in your descendants shall all the families of the earth be blessed."[2] The repeated reference to families underscores God's ongoing blessing of the foundational unit of human society, which is the family. The blessing that God gave to Abraham's family was to be extended to all the nations of the world, and the fundamental channel for the impartation of that blessing was to be the family.

A clear understanding of this truth was central to the Hebrew people who valued their families highly and maintained a high level of respect for parents, spouses, and children. The family was the unit for nurturing and strengthening individuals, as both husbands and wives profited from the balance of their relationship and children were nurtured in the security of a stable, loving environment established in the knowledge of the Lord. The ancient Hebrew home, like the modern Jewish home, was a temple of blessing.

THE CENTER FOR BLESSING

Because the Hebraic family of ancient times viewed their home not merely as a secular social convention but as a holy place, the family became the center for blessing. God's commandment that his blessing be continually bestowed upon the children of Israel[3] was fulfilled not only in the tabernacle and temple but also in the Jewish home when parents assumed the role that was designated for the Aaronic priesthood by imparting the blessing that God commanded upon their children in the way in which God commanded that it be spoken: "This is the way you shall bless the children of Israel. . . ."[4] The blessing has been expanded to include other biblical elements and has become a much-anticipated weekly event in Jewish homes.

The prime importance that the Hebrews attached to domestic life was reinforced by the mutual respect that was maintained between parents and children. Children honored their parents even before doing so became a requirement of the Decalogue[5]; therefore, children placed high value on the favor of their parents. This was especially true of parental blessings which both parents and children believed had profound power to produce good. In Hebrew culture, family blessings were highly prized, even considered the most valuable heritage that parents could bequeath to their children. This is why the author of the apocryphal book of Ecclesiasticus observed that "a father's blessing gives a family firm roots."[6]

The vehicle that God chose for the impartation of his blessing to his children was the Sabbath. It has been said that Israel has not so much kept the Sabbath as the Sabbath has kept Israel.[7] This has been especially true because for the Jewish people, the Sabbath has always been a family celebration. In the Christian world, the one day in seven that has been set apart for God is viewed essentially as an opportunity for corporate worship. The Sabbath among the Jews, however, is first a family exercise that is then expanded into corporate worship. The Jewish Sabbath observance always begins in the home with the family welcoming and celebrating the Sabbath in the security and sanctity of their family temple. Only later is the Sabbath observance extended to the synagogue. It is in the context of family intimacy that meeting, study, prayer, and blessing functions begin to be fulfilled.

God blessed the Sabbath so that it could be a blessed time by setting apart a weekly occasion for blessing in the context of family and community. For millennia, therefore, millions of Jews have anxiously awaited *Shabbat* as a blessing from God that multiplies his blessings. Because *Shabbat* begins on Friday evening at sundown and continues until Saturday evening,[8] the Sabbath is welcomed in the Jewish home at sundown on Friday evening by the entire family. The wife and daughters are given the honor of speaking the blessing and lighting the candles that usher in the Sabbath and welcome God's presence to the family temple.

As the family Sabbath celebration continues, spiritual exercises ensue that include reading God's Word, singing Psalms, and blessing children. The parents, with the father generally taking the leading role, place the blessing that God commanded for the children of Israel on each one of their own children individually. Because Jacob laid his right hand on Ephraim's head when he blessed him, the Jewish father lays his right hand on the head of each child as he speaks the blessing.[9] This blessing involves the combination of both the priestly benediction[10] and other scriptural and personal blessings.[11]

The blessing is introduced by statements that originate in classic biblical blessings. If the child is male, the words that Jacob commanded for the blessing of his descendants: "In your name will Israel pronounce this blessing, 'May God make you like Ephraim and Manasseh.'"[12] If the child is female, the words of the blessing that the leaders of the Israelite community spoke over Ruth are added: "The Lord make you like Sarah and Rebecca, like Rachel and Leah."[13] In this way, each Jewish girl is elevated to the esteemed status of the very women whom God used to establish the Hebrew people and the Israelite nation.

For both boys and girls, then, the blessing begins with the biblical declaration of benediction that was pronounced over their ancestors. These statements connect children with the ancient patriarchs and matriarchs of their faith, building their self-esteem and giving them a sense of context in their extended family community. It invokes importance and accomplishment into their young lives and sets high expectations for their future.

After the initial benedictions, the process continues with the impartation of the blessing that God personally dictated to Moses and ordered to be spoken over all the children of Israel: "The LORD bless you and keep you. The LORD cause his face to shine upon you and be gracious unto you. The LORD turn his face toward you and give you peace."[14] This blessing may also add God's continuing words, "And they shall put my name upon the children of Israel, and I will bless them."[15] In the most ancient times, the priests took this commandment from God literally and actually traced the Hebrew letters for the name of God, יהוה (YHWH), in the forehead or in the right hand of the one who whom they were blessing. The speaking of God's blessing upon children, therefore, is very powerful, for it actually places God's name on them and invokes the promise of God himself, "I will bless them."

Then, parents may employ a personal blessing to speak good things into each child's life, including parental expectations and affirmation of the child's life ambition and the parents' commitment to assist in fulfilling that ambition. Other blessings may be added as well. This is in keeping with the tradition of Jacob, who "blessed [his children], every one with the blessing appropriate to him"[16] by speaking individualized blessings over them. This makes the blessing more than just a routine carried out by rote. It is a personalized blessing that recognizes accomplishment and speaks positive expectations into the life of each child.

In the Christian home, the blessings may continue with the impartation of a request for the sevenfold Spirit of God to be upon each child: "May the Spirit of the LORD rest upon you, the spirit of wisdom, the spirit of understanding, the spirit of counsel, the spirit of strength, the spirit of knowledge, and the spirit of the fear of the LORD."[17] Applying this blessing invokes the seven spirits that burn before God's throne[18] to be manifest in the child's life.

This practice of blessing children is a time-honored Jewish family exercise, part of a continuing emphasis on the value of blessing.[19] The Jewish people take God's command for blessing the children of Israel literally; therefore, they speak his blessing over their own children. In the context of the extended family, the community's teachers also bless their students with the same priestly benediction.[20] The blessing was both a family affair and a part of the community of extended family.

The second part of the family blessing features the husband blessing his wife by speaking, chanting, or singing to her the benediction of Proverbs 31:10-31 for the Woman of Valor: "What a rare find is a capable wife! Her worth is far beyond that of rubies . . . . Many women have done well, but you surpass them all." These words that King Lemuel's[21] mother taught him were declared in the scriptural record itself to be the words of a prophetic oracle,[22] a fact that adds much weight to the blessing. The Jewish people believe that this blessing was originally spoken by Abraham in honor of Sarah and was subsequently transmitted orally through each generation. Whatever the case may be, speaking the Word of God in honor of one's wife is a powerful dynamic. It blesses her. It also establishes her husband's high esteem for her in the eyes of their children. Perhaps even more importantly, it blesses the husband also, for he cannot repeat God's words of blessing upon his wife and children without being blessed himself.

Though it is not generally done in the Jewish home, Christian families may wish to have the wife speak a blessing over the husband. A perfect blessing for this occasion is the declaration of Psalm 112, which is virtually a mirror image of Proverbs 31:10-31. This blessing also builds the esteem of children for their father as they hear their mother blessing him with the words of the Psalmist.

Before the Sabbath evening meal, the father speaks the *Kiddush* blessing, which "sanctifies" (the meaning of *kiddush*— "to make holy") the occasion by praising God for creating the fruit of the vine. As he elevates a cup of wine, he speaks these words: "Blessed are you, O Lord our God, King of the universe, who creates the fruit of the vine." Those who are present then drink a portion of the wine. Then, after the father washes his hands, he speaks this blessing: "Blessed are you, O Lord our God, Ruler of the universe. You have sanctified us with your commandments and enjoined on us the cleansing of the hands." Finally, when all are seated, the father takes two specially prepared loaves of bread, elevates them toward heaven, and makes this declaration: "Blessed are you, O Lord our God, King of the universe, who brings forth bread from the earth," and then shares a portion of the bread with everyone at the table. The bread used in this ceremony is called *challah*. Because the portion of the bread dough that was required to be saved for the priests was called *challah*, partaking of this bread in the home is a holy exercise. Both the blessing for the wine and the blessing for the bread come from antiquity, certainly predating the first century. It is virtually certain that Jesus spoke some form of these blessings at the Last Supper when he blessed God for the bread and the cup.[23]

Blessings After the Meal

After the family shares the Sabbath meal, the father leads in offering the blessings to God after the meal that are called the *Birkat ha-Mazon*.[24] Of all the benedictions in Jewish ritual, this one is considered to be the oldest and most important because it is the first blessing that God specifically commanded all of Israel to practice: "When you have eaten and are full, then you shall bless the LORD your God for the good land which he has given you."[25] In obedience to this instruction, the ancient Israelites prayed and blessed God for their food only after they had eaten, not before. In later times, however, the sages decided that blessings should be said before eating in the context of their belief that nothing that God created for human enjoyment should be experienced without first blessing God who made the provision.[26] The Christian practice of blessing a meal before it is consumed is rooted more in the neo-Platonic idea that material things are not holy and must be blessed before they are consumed or used in a spiritual context. In history, it was also an attempt to pray over food that might have been contaminated in some way.

The *Birkat ha-Mazon* was originally comprised of three blessings: for food, for the land, and for Jerusalem. The blessing for food praises God for feeding all creatures, thereby connecting Israel with all living things.[27] The blessing for the land expresses praise to God for the abundant land of Israel.[28] The blessing for Jerusalem praises God as the "rebuilder" of Zion, thanks him for Jerusalem, and petitions his mercy for Israel.[29] These three blessings long predate the Christian era. A fourth blessing was added in the second century AD when the Jewish people were granted permission to bury their dead after the Romans crushed the revolt that had been led by messianic pretender Bar Kochba. It is a benediction of God who is "kind and deals kindly with all."[30]

The bestowing of blessings continues throughout the Sabbath, featuring both fellowship with family and worship with community. As the day comes to an end, the family again assembles for the *Havdalah* ("separation") experience in which sorrow is expressed for the ending of the Sabbath and aromatic spices are used to carry the sweetness of the Sabbath over into the beginning of the new week.

The entire *Shabbat* experience is one of blessing after blessing. Blessings are imparted that strengthen the family bonds of mutual respect and honor. God is exalted in the context of the home, transforming it from a mere shelter from the elements and a feeding station into a spiritual temple of safety and blessing. In the blessed home, Solomon's observation is true: "A righteous man who walks in his integrity—how blessed are his sons after him."[31]

The impact of family blessings such as these in Jewish homes is immeasurable. When recounting her childhood experiences of being blessed by her rabbi grandfather, Rachel Remen observed, "These few moments were the only time in my week when I felt completely safe and at rest."[32] If this were the only effect of the blessing, it would be reason enough for parents to bestow it on their children. The truth is, however, that family blessings have life-giving and lifelong benefits.

SPECIAL BLESSING OCCASIONS

Significant events in the life cycle of each person are occasions for blessing. This is especially true in the development of a child. Blessing should begin with the time when conception has occurred to the end of the parent's allotted time on earth. Parents should never cease to bless their children. Parents can speak words of blessing over the unborn child in its mother's womb. The blessing can petition divine protection and favor on both mother and child. Immediately after the birth of a child, parents can bless their newborn.

In the Jewish community every son experiences the covenant of circumcision on the eighth day of his life. Christians can profit from this example by verbally blessing their infant children either through a form of baptism[33] or through infant dedication.[34] Parents have a significant opportunity to bless their children when they reach puberty and assume responsibility for their own actions. In Judaism, this experience is called *Bar Mitzvah* ("Son of the Commandment"). In many communities, this practice is also extended to girls in the *Bat Mitzvah* ("Daughter of the Commandment"). It is at the age of thirteen (twelve for girls) when the child assumes responsibility for his or her own life. In the ceremony, the father publicly acknowledges that from this time forward he is no longer responsible for the child's actions. This practice is likely the source of the Christian idea of the "age of accountability," the age at which children are considered to have become responsible before God for their own actions. Though the concept of the "age of accountability" is rooted in Isaiah 7:16: ". . . before the child knows to reject evil and choose what is right," identifying this age with puberty arises from rabbinic tradition.[35]

Puberty is a significant event, a rite of passage in the life of a young person. At this time, profound biological, physiological, and chemical changes take place impacting both the body and the spirit of children. Christians can recognize this important time by publicly blessing their children and recognizing and affirming their transition from childhood and dependency on their parents to responsibility and maturity. A special blessing in addition to the weekly family *Shabbat* blessings can be spoken over the child to encourage the youngster at this rite of passage and affirm parental support as the child makes decisions for life.[36]

Another of the most important events in an individual's life is marriage, the making of a covenant with another person to join in unity and share life together. It is the time of the making of a new family, a new home. The bride and groom should carefully and prayerfully involve their parents in this exercise. Since, in ancient times, parents even chose mates for their children, surely children today should look to their parents for advice and counsel in what is one of life's most important decisions and should speak their parental blessing into the lives of their children when they are married.

Then, children should want their parents to be involved in the ceremony that joins them covenantally with their mate. This is a significant opportunity for parents of both the bride and the groom to pronounce God's blessing and their own personal blessings over their children. The ceremony of marriage is enriched by the participation of parents in fulfilling the one role that is assigned to them for life: blessing their children. The biblical blessing should be used, and additional blessings may be written into the liturgy for the event, or they may be given extemporaneously.

MORE BLESSINGS

As children become adults, they have the privilege of continuing to receive their parents' blessings. There is never an age when they outgrow the blessing. Jacob was still blessing his adult sons when he was advanced in age. At the same time, however, children have the opportunity to rise up and call their parents blessed,[37] to honor their father and mother[38] both in word and deed and to reciprocate the blessings that they have received from their parents by blessing them in turn.

The point in time when one reaches full age and is ready to be "gathered to his ancestors"[39] is an important occasion for the intimacy of the family to be manifest in blessing. A patriarch or matriarch will want to add God's blessing to children and grandchildren and to hear words of blessing from their most precious loved ones as they face the unknown but certain experience of death, burial, and resurrection.

Family blessing, then, is a lifetime affair. A blessed family never misses an opportunity for blessing one another. Family blessing is the heritage from the Lord, who is the source of all the blessings that believers can experience in their family temple.

BLESSING BY FAITH

Because Christians have not been accustomed to the biblical function of the home as the center for spiritual growth, they are often uncomfortable with assuming the role of blessing. Their codependency upon the clergy as the official channel of blessing has robbed them of this privilege. In many cases, the church has eviscerated the home of this, its most important function. Those who have come to realize the extent of their impoverishment through the loss of this important part of Christianity's Hebraic heritage can now reclaim their rights and privileges.

Generational inhibitions, however, can restrict the freedom to engage in what is clearly a parental responsibility. Because one's parents have not fulfilled this role is no excuse for one's not taking on the challenge. Because one is not fluent in verbal expression is also not an excuse. Perhaps what is really needed is the faith to bless. When discussing the subject of faith, most Christians' attention goes immediately to Hebrews 11, the one chapter in the Apostolic Scriptures that is often referred to as the "Roll Call of Faith." Here men and women of amazing faith are listed, along with some of the astounding results of their faith. There is Enoch who walked so closely with God that he was translated directly to God's presence so as not to experience death. There is Noah who built an ark and saved humanity from the flood. There are Abraham and Sarah who, in their old age, experienced the miraculous birth of Isaac. There is Moses who delivered the Israelites from Egyptian bondage through astounding miracles. There are Gideon, Samson, David, and Samuel, all of whom witnessed supernatural intervention on behalf of the nation of Israel.

In the midst of all these miracles and astounding accomplishments, however, two men are mentioned simply because they had the faith to bless their children and grandchildren: "*By faith* Isaac blessed Jacob and Esau in regard to their future . . . . *By faith* Jacob, when he was dying, blessed each of Joseph's sons."[40] The faith that both Isaac and Jacob exhibited was equal with the faith that routed armies, divided the Red Sea, preserved Noah's ark, and established prophets' words. It was faith that inspired these men to propel their values like arrows into the following generations in the form of blessings for their children and grandchildren.[41]

Should Christians who are filled with the Holy Spirit not have faith of the same quality that both Isaac and Jacob manifest? Perhaps it is time to take the faith with which one believes to move mountains and begin with the blessing of children. It may seem like a leap of faith for some, but it is merely a step of obedience to God's command: "Bless the children of Israel." Without such a step of faith, one will experience the sorrow that Rachel Remen's mother noted when asked why she had not blessed her daughter: "I have blessed you every day of your life. . . . I just never had the wisdom to do it out loud."[42]

Fixed forms of blessing that the Jewish people have used for generations may be shared in the context of Christian families. Self-composed or spontaneous expressions may also be used. If nothing else, as a Christian, be Christlike: let it be said of you that you "took [your] children up in your arms, laid [your] hands on them, and blessed them,"[43] as Jesus did with the children who came to him. Whatever the case, by all means—and by faith—bless your children. Remember to follow the piety and priorities of King David, the man after God's own heart who, after dancing before the Ark of the Covenant with all his might, returned to his own family temple so that he could bless his family.

Outline for Family Blessings

When you as a Christian family gather together in your family temple for the time set apart for God and family, you may wish to use the following outline as a guide for blessing both God and your family. This formula is similar to what has been done in Jewish homes for centuries. Language is added that expands the exercise to include various Christian themes.

At sundown, the mother may light candles and make the following blessing:

"Blessed are you, O Lord our God, King of the universe, who has

sanctified us by your Word and has called us to be a light unto our world. We thank you for your Son our Lord, Jesus the Christ, who has illuminated our lives with his divine presence and has given us eternal life."

The parents, with the father generally taking the leading role, now place the blessing that God commanded to be spoken over the children of Israel on each of their children. The priestly benediction is introduced by scriptural blessings appropriate to sons and daughters. Parents may lay their hands on the head of each child individually and make the following blessing:

"May the Lord make you like Ephraim and Manasseh" (if the child is a boy).

"May the Lord make you like Rachel and Leah, like Sarah and Rebecca" (if the child is a girl).

The blessing continues with this scripturally mandated personal blessing from God:

"The LORD *bless you and keep you. The* LORD *make his face shine upon you and be gracious unto you. The* LORD *lift up his countenance upon you and give you peace."*

You may continue:

"With this blessing, God said, 'You will put my name upon the children of Israel, and I will bless them.' "

Now, as Jacob did centuries ago, you should speak into each child's life a personal blessing that is appropriate to the child. This can express your praise for the child's accomplishment as well as your expectations for the child's future. This should amplify the child's vision and ambition for life.

The blessing can now continue with the invocation of the sevenfold Spirit of God upon the child:

"May the Spirit of God rest upon you, the spirit of wisdom, the spirit of understanding, the spirit of counsel, the spirit of might, the spirit of knowledge, and the spirit of the fear of the LORD. *And may you always delight in the fear of the* LORD."

Next, the husband blesses the wife by reading or reciting all or part of Proverbs 31:10-31:

"A wife of noble character who can find? She is worth far more than rubies. Her husband has full confidence in her and lacks nothing of value. She brings him good, not harm, all the days of her life. . . . She sets about her work vigorously. . . . She opens her arms to the poor and extends her hands to the needy. . . . Her husband is respected at the city gate, where he takes his seat among the elders of the land. . . . She speaks with wisdom, and faithful instruction is on her tongue. She watches over the affairs of her household and does not eat the bread of idleness. Her children arise and call her blessed; her husband also, and he praises her: 'Many women do noble things, but you surpass them all.' Charm is deceptive and beauty is fleeting; but a woman who fears the LORD *is to be praised. Give her the reward she has earned, and let her works bring her praise at the city gate."*

The wife may also bless her husband by reading or reciting Psalm 112:1-9:

"Blessed is the man who fears the LORD, *who finds great delight in his commands. His children will be mighty in the land; the generation of the upright will be blessed. Wealth and riches are in his house, and his righteousness endures forever. Even in darkness light dawns for the upright, for the gracious and compassionate and righteous man. Good will come to him who is generous and lends freely, who conducts his affairs with justice. Surely he will never be shaken; a righteous man will be remembered forever. He will have no fear of bad news; his heart is steadfast, trusting in the* LORD. *His heart is secure, he will have no fear; in the end he will look in triumph on his foes. He has scattered abroad his gifts to the poor, his righteousness endures forever; his horn will be lifted high in honor."*

Before the meal, the father takes a cup of grape juice or wine and makes the *Kiddush* blessing that Jesus and the apostles made:

"Blessed are you, O Lord our God, King of the universe, who has created the fruit of the vine." He may continue: *"We thank you for the blood of your Son that cleanses us from all iniquity."*

Each member of the family partakes of the fruit of the

fine.

In like manner, the father takes two specially prepared loaves of bread and speaks another blessing that Jesus made:

"Blessed are you, O Lord our God, King of the universe, who brings forth bread from the earth." He may continue: *"We thank you for your Son, the bread of life from heaven who strengthens our souls."*

Each family member eats a portion of the bread.

Afterwards, the family shares the Sabbath meal together. In the course of the meal, they may discuss the significance of the foods on the table that date from Bible times: bread, wine, oil, and salt, all of which have great spiritual significance. During this time, the family may join in singing and sharing of God's Word.

When the meal is concluded, the family may join in blessing God for the foods. This is in obedience to God's command that the children of Israel were to bless the Lord after they had eaten and were full.[44] The following *Birkhat ha-Mazon* blessing dates from before the time of Jesus:

The father says: *"Let us say grace."* The rest of the family responds: *"Blessed be the Name of the Lord from this time forth and for ever."* The father continues: *"We will bless him of whose bounty we have partaken."* The family responds: *"Blessed be he of whose bounty we have partaken and through whose goodness we live."*

The family together may say all or part of the following blessing:

"Blessed are you, O Lord our God, King of the universe, who feeds the whole world with your goodness, with grace, with loving kindness and tender mercy; you give food to all flesh, for your loving kindness endures for ever. Through your great goodness we have never lacked food: O may we never lack it for ever and ever for your great Name's sake, since you nourish and sustain all beings, and do good unto all, and provide food for all your creatures whom you have created. Blessed are you, O Lord, who gives food to all.

*"We thank you, O Lord our God, because you gave as an heritage
unto our fathers a desirable, good, and ample land . . . and for the food
wherewith you do constantly feed and sustain us on every day, in every
season, at every hour. For all this, O Lord our God, we thank and bless
you. Blessed be your Name by the mouth of all living continually and for
ever, even as it is written, And you shall eat and be satisfied, and you shall
bless the Lord your God for the good land which he has given you. Blessed
are you, O Lord, for the land and for the food.*

*"Have mercy, O Lord our God, upon Israel your people, upon Jerusa-
lem your city, upon Zion the abiding place of your glory, upon the kingdom
of the house of David, and upon the great and holy house that was called
by your Name. O Lord our God, our Father, feed us, nourish us, sustain,
support and relieve us, and speedily, O Lord our God, grant us relief from
all our troubles. We beseech you, O Lord our God, let us not be in need
either of the gifts of mortals or of their loans, but only of your helping
hand, which is full, open, holy, and ample, so that we may never be put to
shame or humiliated. And rebuild Jerusalem the holy city speedily in our
days. Blessed are you, O Lord, who in your compassion rebuilds Jerusalem.
Amen."*

The family may conclude by praying the Lord's Prayer, after
which the father may say, *"Now, may the grace of our Lord Jesus
Christ, the love of God, and the fellowship of the Holy Spirit be with us
all. Amen."*

This concludes the *Erev Shabbat* (Sabbath evening) family
blessing exercise.

Outline for Blessing a Child at Puberty

In addition to the usual *Shabbat* blessing for children, you
may speak these words over your child: *"We bless you in the name
of the Lord as you make this important transition in life. May you ever
hide God's Word in your heart so you do not sin against him. As you now
take responsibility for your own actions before God, we will stand with you
and assist you in fulfilling your vision for life. May you ever live in the*

richest of God's blessings."

OUTLINE FOR A WEDDING BLESSING

You may say these words over your daughter the bride: *"What a rare gift is a capable wife! She is worth far more than rubies. May your husband put his full confidence in you and never lack anything of value. May you bring him good all the days of your life. May you always be strong and your health be vigorous so that you may watch over the affairs of your home. May your arms always be extended to the poor and the needy. May you be clothed with strength and dignity. May God give you wisdom, and may faithful instruction be always on your tongue. Many women have done well, but may you surpass them all. You have been a treasure to us, a gift and a heritage from the Lord. We are thankful that God entrusted us with your life and has allowed us to nurture you unto this time. As you now join with your beloved to create a new home, we bless you with all the blessings of heaven and earth. May the Lord answer you when you are in distress. May he remember your sacrifices and give you the desires of your heart. May you enjoy the fruit of your labor and may prosperity and blessing be yours. May the Lord bless you all the days of your life, and may you live to bless and enjoy your children's children."*

You may say these words over your son, the groom: *"Blessed is the man who fears the Lord, who delights greatly in his commandments. The generations that follow you will be blessed because of your goodness. May you be gracious to your wife and full of compassion. May you never be afraid. Let your heart always be steadfast, trusting in the Lord. May you always remember to give to the poor and conduct your affairs generously and with justice so that wealth and riches may be in your own house. You have been a treasure to us, a gift and a heritage from the Lord. We are thankful that God entrusted us with your life and has allowed us to nurture you unto this time. As you now join with your beloved to create a new home, we bless you with all the blessings of heaven and earth. May the Lord answer you when you are in distress. May he remember your sacrifices and give you the desires of your heart. May you enjoy the fruit of your labor and may prosperity and blessing be yours. May the Lord bless you all the days of your life, and may you live to bless and enjoy your children's children."*

[1] Genesis 12:2-3.
[2] Genesis 28:14, NASV.
[3] Numbers 6:24-28.
[4] Numbers 6:23; Genesis 48:20.
[5] Exodus 20:12.
[6] Ecclesiasticus (Sirach) 3:9.
[7] Ahad Ha-Am, quoted in Eliot N. Dorff, *For the Love of God and People: A Philosophy of Jewish Law* (Philadelphia: Jewish Publication Society, 2007), p. 178.
[8] In biblical terms, the day begins at sundown so that evening precedes morning and a day is defined as "evening and morning," even as the biblical creation narrative declares (cf. Genesis 1:5).
[9] Genesis 48:14.
[10] Numbers 6:23-26.
[11] Genesis 49:28, NASV.
[12] Genesis 48:20.
[13] Ruth 4:11.
[14] Numbers 6:23-26.
[15] Numbers 6:27.
[16] Genesis 49:2-28.
[17] Isaiah 11:2.
[18] Revelation 4:5.
[19] It is uncertain how ancient the Jewish practice of blessing children may be. Its earliest mention in extant literature is in *Brautspiegel*, a book published in Basel in 1602. The writer stresses the fact that children should be trained from infancy to value parental blessings: "Before the children can walk they should be carried on Sabbath and holidays to the father and mother to be blessed; after they are able to walk they shall go of their own accord with bowed body and shall incline their heads and receive the blessing." See Moses Henochs, *Brautspiegel*, quoted in "Blessing of Children," Jewish Encyclopedia.com. p. 3.
[20] In *Synagoga Judaica*, published in 1604, Buxtorf notes that on Sabbath parents bless their children and teachers bless their pupils.
[21] It is thought that Lemuel may well have been a term of endearment for Solomon himself.
[22] Proverbs 31:1.
[23] Matthew 26:26-27.
[24] *Mazon* means "foods."
[25] Deuteronomy 8:10.
[26] Babylonian Talmud, *Berakoth* 35a.
[27] The first blessing is attributed by some traditions to Moses. See Babylonian Talmud, *Berakhot* 48b.

[28] The second blessing of the *Birkat ha-Mazon* is attributed by the sages to Joshua.

[29] The third blessing of the *Birkat ha-Mazon* is attributed to David by the rabbis.

[30] The fourth blessing of the *Birkat ha-Mazon* is attributed to Solomon by the sages. It is not considered to be Toraitic as are the first three.

[31] Proverbs 20:7, NASV.

[32] Rachel Naomi Remen, *My Grandfather's Blessing* (New York: Riverdale Books, 2002), p. 48.

[33] While infant baptism has long been controversial in the Christian church, the fact that Paul equates baptism with circumcision in Colossians 2:11-12 lends support to those who wish to engage in baptismal rites for their infant children.

[34] Others may wish to present their children in their spiritual community for dedication as was the case with Samuel in 1 Samuel 1:24ff.

[35] S. Michael Houdmann, *Got Questions?* (Enumclaw, WA: Winepress Publishing, 2009), p. 119.

[36] See John D. Garr, *Blessings for Family and Friends* (Atlanta: Golden Key Press, 2010) for recommended blessings for all occasions.

[37] Proverbs 31:28.

[38] Exodus 20:12.

[39] Genesis 49:29.

[40] Hebrews 11:20-21, emphasis added.

[41] Psalm 127:4.

[42] Rachel Naomi Remen, p. 88.

[43] Mark 10:16.

[44] Deuteronomy 8:10.

Chapter 11

The Family Ethos

ESTABLISHING SECURE FAMILY BORDERS

In order to function with integrity and safety, each home must establish its own family ethos, its own family ethics, and its own family etiquette. Individuals stand before God for themselves and must answer to God according to the dictates of their consciences that have been tuned to God's Word; therefore, they must have their own individual code of ethics. In similar manner, families must have their own standards based on their collective sensibilities and ethical standards. Because the family is made up of more than one individual, the family's ethos, ethics, and etiquette must be established by careful and thoughtful interaction between husband and wife and then with listening ears sensitive to the heart's cry of their children. Finally, in a larger sense, the standards for conduct of a community must be established through prayerful dialogue among all the members of the community as together they consider God's Word and its proper application in the context of their cultural distinctives.

While certain infallible, general rules for human conduct are constant because they are specifically delineated in the Holy Scriptures, and these rules can never be compromised for any cultural reason, there are countless areas where great flexibility based on the traditions and sensibilities of different people groups can and should be accommodated. This is not to indicate that the moral and ethical standards of individuals, families, and communities are situational, based in the perverse consequentialism of postmodernity, for situational ethics breed chaos and the violation of divine imperatives. It is to say, however, that individuals, families, and communities have the God-given right and responsibility to express the principles of God's Word in ways that are culturally and esthetically appropriate for them. One culture is not superior over another. God's rules for proper human conduct in relationship to himself and to others are constant and immutable; therefore, it is the task of individuals, families, and communities to define the manner in which these divine principles should be contextualized in their own situation.

In the Jewish community, the standards for conduct of individuals, families, and communities have been delineated under the rubric of *halakhah*, the way in which one should walk. *Halakhah* is, therefore, very important in Judaism and among the Jewish people. Taken from the Hebrew word הָלַךְ (*halak*, meaning "to walk"), *halakhah* describes the established norm for proper conduct in a community. It literally means "a prescribed manner of living" and is used to define the Jewish lifestyle. As Edward Queen notes "the process of developing self-awareness, self-assertion, and self-creativity . . . is made possible through the halacha, the religious law that regulates personal, social, and ritual conduct. Only through halacha is 'the apprehension and fulfillment of God's will' possible."[1]

Generally speaking, *halakhah* is an outline of standards for human actions in specific situations that have been determined by the spiritual leaders of Jewish communities. These findings are based on rabbinic interpretation of both the Torah (the Pentateuch) and oral tradition (called the "Oral Torah") which has been codified in the Talmud (composed of commentaries upon the Torah called the *Mishnah*[2] and commentaries on the *Mishnah* called the *Gemara*[3]). *Halakhah*, then, is an effort to provide guidelines for roles and boundaries for Jewish individuals, for Jewish families, and for Jewish communities. *Halakhah* defines what is required to be a practitioner of Judaism and a member in good standing of the Jewish community.

The Talmud defines roles for men, women, and children in a monumental corpus of literature that has been developed through centuries of rabbinic dialogue, disputation, and formulation. The Talmud has been highly valued because it has been a boundary-defining mechanism that has constructed a "fence around the Torah," warning of impending violation of God's commandments if one ventures beyond its borders.[4] Through *halakhah* of the Talmud, boundaries are established within which Jewish people can function without fear of violating the Torah's instructions.

Christian families can well profit from understanding the principle of *halakhah* that are used in the Jewish community. First, the church in its various communions should (and does) define roles for men, women, and children and for leaders and laypersons in the community of faith. Both leaders and laity should collaborate in defining what is considered acceptable conduct within the communities. At the same time, however, the *halakhah* principle should also be manifest in the home, so that each family, within the guidelines of its constituent community, should determine standards for acceptable conduct within the home. Boundaries are secure borders that limit the incursion of damaging forces into the safety of the family temple.

CONFUSION AND BROKEN FENCES

In modern society, secularism and atheism have purposely blurred both roles and boundaries for human interpersonal relationships, especially as they concern to the home. It is increasingly important, therefore, for Christian families to

assume their God-given responsibility to function within the
context of the roles that God has established for husbands,
wives, fathers, mothers, and children. Christian families must
also establish and maintain boundaries for what is considered
proper ethical and social conduct in their homes. Going with the
societal flow down the broad road will lead to disintegration and
destruction of the most precious earthly thing that believers
have—their family relationships.

The atheistic secular mind has purposely sought to confuse
masculine and feminine roles, all in the name of liberating women.
At the same time, it has carefully and systematically inculcated
the concepts of consequentialism or situational ethics, which
fundamentally are not ethics at all because they recognize no
absolutes. Generations of children have been reared (actually
"raised" like soybeans or corn) in an environment lacking clear
gender role models and void of the moral compass of absolutes
ethics. This violence against the body politic of society has crept
with treacherous subtlety into the church and synagogue, influ-
encing the thinking of both of the communities that have been
commissioned to be God's light to the world.[5]

The overwhelming onslaught of political correctness has
demanded that everyone in society conform to its demand for
the homogenization of society and the destruction of antiquated
biblical mores. All of this has been very subtly introduced in the
name of tolerance. "I'm ok, you're ok" and "I have my truth;
you have your truth" have become the mantras of political correctness. Christians have been swept along in this tide of deceit and
perversion, and have compromised the fundamental concepts of
their faith because of a frantic need to be seen as tolerant toward
the "rights" of others. The fundamental tenets of both Judaism
and Christianity have been rejected by postmodern societies that
are hell-bent on dragging everyone into their gulag of corruption
and debauchery. For them, everything goes—everything, that is,

except the God of the Jews and his restrictive laws aimed at bridling the rebellious heart of humankind.

Because of the incursion of godless humanism into the church, Christian homes now experience a divorce rate that is as great as or greater than that of society in general. Christian men and women no longer have a clear sense of self-identity and purpose. They do not understand their roles. They no longer insist on biblical morality, allowing their standards to be set by the entertainment industry through ubiquitous music, television, and social media. If a popular movie or music idol does something, it must not be all that bad. "Have we just been too old fashioned?" parents wonder. "After all, God *is* love." As a result of this kind of mentality, the church has become so worldly and the world has become so churchy that it is increasingly difficult to tell the difference.

What are parents who have not been totally blinded by societal attacks upon their roles and boundaries to do? The answer is a "back-to-the-Bible" movement. The old book that everyone thought was an outdated myth is the answer, the most up-to-date manual for human behavior that exists in the world. When believers return to the Holy Scriptures they find the answers to life's questions. And it is far more important to be biblically correct than it is to be politically correct—not to mention the eternal consequences.!

In order for the Bible to be rightly applied, however, it must be interpreted in the light of the culture and history of the people to whom and through whom it was given. The Bible is a Jewish book and can be understood only with a Jewish mindset and worldview. This is in keeping with the grammatico-historical hermeneutic, the most ancient and sound Christian methodology for biblical interpretation that was revived in the sixteenth-century Protestant Reformation. Interpreting Holy Scripture through the lenses of cultures that are foreign to the book and its fundamental premises has resulted in perverted teachings that have produced the opposite of biblical intent. It is from these aberrant religious concepts that societies have sought relief, swinging the conceptual pendulum to the extremes of total secularization.

Redefining biblically Hebraic roles for family members could never be more important than at this time. Likewise, establishing clear biblical boundaries for ethical conduct and proper interpersonal relationships could never be more essential than now. In the face of the subtle attack of Satan on the very foundation of society's social fabric, it is important that Christians return to doing God's thing God's way. To do less or more is to invite further disintegration of the family.

BIBLICAL ROLES

Despite secularist efforts to impose this unisex view of humanity on postmodern culture, there is a difference between men and women! Masculinity is masculinity, and femininity is femininity. Men are men, and women are women. Attempts by sociological revisionism to blur psychological lines by insisting that men discover their feminine side and women assert their masculine side have not resulted in the emergence of a physical androgyne, the perfect hermaphrodite. If there is no difference between male and female, why are millions of dollars spent annually on sonograms in order to determine as early as possible the gender of a fetus? And, why at a baby's birth are its genitalia the first anatomical parts that are examined so that its gender can be confirmed? Yes, there is a physical difference, and there are mental, psychological, and emotional differences as well. These differences are in no way demeaning to either male or female, nor do they make either one inferior or subject to the other. They are simply differences and distinctives that God intended to be complementary and counterbalancing.[6]

When either males or females are forced to develop their

self-identities in what they are not, turmoil results. When men are forced into feminine roles and women are forced into masculine roles, confusion breeds uncertainty and emotional instability. Male and female acceptance of biblical roles brings honor to God and establishes healthy foundations for joyful, successful living. Since personality can only reveal itself in persons, it is "specifically in human nature—in man and woman—that we see God."[7] The image of God is the image that is manifest in male and female: "God created humanity in his own image . . . male and female created he them."[8] God made humanity as male and female, both of whom were necessary for the full manifestation of the divine image and likeness. If God had intended to create masculinized femininity or feminized masculinity, he would not have created the first humans as male and female in the first place. When husbands determine to be fully male and wives determine to be fully female within the context of gender-role parameters established in the Holy Scriptures, marriage and family are strengthened by the divinely ordained counterbalance that is holistic and healthy.

Roles, like boundaries, can only be worked out in detail in the context of home and community. No specific blueprint for human personality can be forced upon each individual. Even in discussing biblical roles, one can only speak in generalities and of norms. Each individual is different and will find fulfillment only in a personalized and contextualized manifestation of the general principles that the Scriptures describe. This process is the same for cultural applications of biblical concepts in the larger communities of faith. Divine principles may not be compromised or syncretized with human or satanic ideas; however, they must be contextualized in the indigenous cultures in which they are manifest. Otherwise, individuals and groups will be required to be what they are not.

Various personality types will interrelate in different ways in marriage, family, and community. This underscores the importance

of communicating and establishing realistic expectations both
for roles and boundaries in each individual marriage and family.
Extroverts, introverts, and ambiverts will relate to one another
in different manners and to varying degrees. Analytical, driver,
amiable, and expressive personality types will relate to one another in various ways. Some are born or trained leaders; others
are followers. Most are somewhere in between. It is important,
therefore, that each community and ultimately each family work
out its own roles and boundaries within the context of biblically
Hebraic guidelines and neither impose its own ethos on the
community nor allow the community to impose its ethos on
them. As Hillel said, "Do not judge your fellow until you are in
his place."[9] This provides a framework wherein each family can
be led by the Holy Spirit and not straitjacketed into some form
or ritual by the constraints of systems imposed upon them by a
larger community.[10]

SETTING SECURE BOUNDARIES

Boundary definition is an essential part of a family's ethos
or *halakhah*. Beyond outlining proper roles for family members,
secure boundaries must be established for every home. The individual family has considerable help in this matter, for the Holy
Scriptures have circumscribed human existence with many very
clear borders. One need only look in the Bible to find the Creator's
design and maintenance specifications. Each family should be
unreservedly committed to the divine inspiration, absolute authority, and clear reliability of the Bible as the guidebook for
human existence. When parents have recognized it as the source
for absolutes, establishing boundaries is greatly facilitated.

Secondary assistance in family *halakhah* is found in worshipping communities. There is wisdom in Solomon's observation that
"where no wise direction is, people fall; but in the multitude of
counsellors there is safety."[11] The wise king also noted that "plans

fail for lack of counsel, but with many advisers they succeed."[12] It is simply wise for families to seek the input of a trusted community of believers into their personal and familial lives. Corporate leaders in the body of Christ are commissioned with the responsibility of establishing *halakhah* for those in their charge.[13] Jesus required the people to observe the instructions of those who sat "in Moses' seat," the spiritual leaders of the Jewish community.[14] Believers will remember and even obey leaders who have spoken God's Word to them and have demonstrated righteousness through their godly lifestyles.[15]

Guidelines may vary from community to community and from ethnicity to ethnicity, for the divine principles of Scripture must be contextualized into every corporate situation. This is the reason that God has given latitude for expression and fulfillment of his purposes. Paul most eloquently described this divine pluriformity by noting that various members of the Christian fellowship were at liberty to function in different ways, but no one was to judge another.[16] As Paul observed, each individual (and family) must be "fully persuaded in his own mind."[17] What may be considered acceptable etiquette in one place may be entirely unacceptable elsewhere. It is important, therefore, that families conform as much as possible to the lifestyles of their communities as long as those lifestyles do not violate the clear instructions of Holy Scripture.[18] True unity in the community of faith is that which maintains cohesion while encouraging diversity. Individual families should, however, remember Hillel's advice: "Do not separate yourself from the community. Do not be too sure of yourself until the day of your death."[19] Isolation from the community of believers is an invitation to deception and disaster.

Beyond those things in family life that are specifically addressed by the Word of God and in addition to suggestions for proper behavior in a specific community, there are other aspects of family life that must be judged, set forth, and maintained within the confines of the family. Parents together must determine what is acceptable deportment within their own family. They must live by their own rules first. Then they must teach their children conformity to these guidelines, enforcing family decorum. Again, these family preferences can be wide and varied, as long as they do not violate biblical precepts. What one family may be convicted to do may not be the same as what another family may consider essential. As with tolerance for congregational differences on protocols, diversities of emphases in various families must be respected and honored.

Just as Israel's deliverance was effected one family at a time with a lamb for each household,[20] so each family must take responsibility for its own spiritual condition and its fulfillment of the things of God. Like Judah in Nehemiah's time, each family must build the part of the corporate wall of protection that is in front of its own house.[21] Security in the family temple results from having constructed solid fortifications, establishing parameters and perimeters for right conduct within the home that shut out incursions of foreign and injurious elements from without. Boundaries of family *halakhah* help make the home sanctuary a true retreat to safety and sanctity.

Commitment to God's Word with family *halakhah* builds a hedge of defense around the home. The living Word becomes a sentinel at the gate of the family temple, much like the *mezuzah* that stands guard duty at the doors of Jewish homes because they have literally fulfilled God's command and have written his instructions on the doorposts of their homes. Family *halakhah* guards the gates, providing security for the family within and protection from the enemy without.

ESTABLISHING *HALAKHAH*

Family *halakhah* is vital to the family temple. The right and responsibility of each family to establish its own ethos must be both respected and encouraged. First, it allows the home to be the locus for spiritual development as it was designed to be. Second, it keeps family members from abdicating their own responsibilities in favor of community leaders. Third, it promotes commitment to the individual family from all its members, both parents and children. Fourth, it encourages maturity in that it requires individual responsibility and accountability. Fifth, it positions each family for its own face-to-face encounter with God, a return to the Edenic sanctuary.

Joshua summed up the beauty and strength of proper attendance to family *halakhah* this way: "As for me and my house, we will serve the LORD."[22] In the final analysis, it is a family-by-family decision. The way in which one should walk is established in the lifestyle that is lived in the family temple, family ethos.

[1] Edward L. Queen, II, Stephen R. Prothero, and Gardner H. Shatuck, eds., *Encyclopedia of American Religious History Set* (New York: Infobase Publishing, 1996), p. 940.

[2] The *Mishnah* (from the verb *shanah*, meaning "to study and review,) is the third-century redaction of the debates between the sages known as the Tannaim who lived between the first century BC and the second century AD. The effort of the *Mishnah* was to "build a fence around the Torah" by establishing the way in which the Jewish people should conduct heir lives.

[3] The *Gemara* (from the Aramaic word *gamar*, meaning "to study or learn by tradition"), is a commentary on the *Mishnah* featuring the analysis that completes the Talmud from the discussions of the *Amoraim*, scholars who lived between the third and fifth centuries AD. In fact, there are two Gemaras and, hence, two Talmuds. One was developed in Tiberias and Caesarea, Israel, (called the *Yerushalmi*), and the other developed in Babylon (called the *Bavli*).

[4] The opening words of the *Mishnah* are these from the tractate *Pirkei Avot* (Chapters of the Fathers): "Be deliberate in judgment, raise up many disciples, and build a fence around the Torah."

[5] Isaiah 42:6; Matthew 5:14.

[6] For a thorough and comprehensive study of the counterbalancing complementarity of male and female, see John D. Garr, *Coequal and Counterbalanced: God's Blueprint for Women and Men* (Atlanta, GA: Golden Key Press, 2012).

[7] Steven G. Post, "Splendor of Love," in *Nature, Man, and God* (Dallas: Southern Methodist University Press, 1994), p. 17.

[8] Genesis 1:27.

[9] Hillel, *Mishnah, Pirkei Avot* 2:5.

[10] The imposition of a standard for conduct upon any individual that is not specifically delineated in Holy Scripture is a form of legalism regardless as to the denomination or religious community that attempts to make such an imposition.

[11] Proverbs 11:14, Jewish Publication Society Old Testament.

[12] Proverbs 15:22, New International Version.

[13] When Jesus said in Matthew 16:19 that whatever his disciples bound or loosed on earth would be bound or loosed in heaven, he was affirming their authority to bind upon or loose from believers those requirements that would benefit their spiritual lives. This was the same authority that Jesus recognized in the scribes and Pharisees who established Jewish *halakhah*.

[14] Matthew 23:2-3.

[15] Hebrews 13:7,17.

[16] Romans 14:4-14.

[17] Romans 14:4.

[18] Families should avoid assembling in corporate fellowships where clear biblical teachings are being violated. Not insisting on family *halakhah* in these situations is to invite being drawn into a cult and opening the family boundaries to all sorts of deception.

[19] Hillel, *Mishnah, Pirkei Avot* 2.5. See Steven Carr Reuben, *Raising Jewish Children in a Contemporary World* (Rocklin, Calif.: Prima Publishing, 1992), p. 145.

[20] Exodus 12:3.

[21] Nehemiah 3:1-32.

[22] Joshua 24:15.

Chapter 12

Marriage and the Family Temple

THE FOUNDATION OF THE FAMILY TEMPLE

Marriage is perhaps one of the least understood institutions in today's world. This most intimate of interpersonal relationships has been grounded more in the ideas of pagan philosophers than in the teaching of Hebrew prophets and apostles. The results could hardly be more disastrous for the well-being of society. In order to put things right in the understanding of the home, it is important to begin with the institution that creates a home in the first place. Marriage must be returned to the biblically Hebraic matrix from which it emerged.

Marriage was instituted by God himself in Eden. It was the divine design for human companionship and for the perpetuation of the human species. God joined Adam and Eve together as one and commanded that all subsequent human beings find their mate and be likewise joined in marital congress.[1] Marriage is the process of reuniting separated male and female genders into one superentity. It is a return to the wholeness of oneness. It is the fulfillment of the divine command that children leave their parents and become joined together in covenantal unity[2] so that they can fulfill the first divine injunction: "Be fruitful and multiply and fill the earth.[3] It is the highest and holiest interpersonal relationship that is possible for human beings. Erasmus declared, "Much reverence is due [marriage] which was instituted by God [before all else]. The rest were instituted upon earth, but this in paradise. The rest for a remedy, this for partnership in happiness."[4]

Marriage has always been the legitimate order for human intimacy and procreation. Those who would join themselves together physically must first join themselves in a covenantal relationship, a lifelong commitment to fidelity. The form and order of this agreement may vary widely; however, the divine principle of covenant is inviolable. Any consummation of intimacy outside this boundary is illegitimate and sinful, in violation of divine commandments.[5]

By making a marriage covenant before God, husband and wife create a holy sanctuary wherein they are privileged to share in God's creative work by sustaining human life and making it holy, thereby perpetuating the image and likeness of God in the earth. The traditional marriage ceremony in Judaism features the exchange of a ring and the declaration: "Behold, you are consecrated unto me by this ring." Christian weddings feature similar words that create a state of holiness (separation) in which life can be wholly embraced. For the couple who are thus consecrated to one another, the rest of humanity disappears, forsaken for the sanctity of their union in their family temple.

God expressed his concern that his children respect the sanctity of marriage when he declared, "The wife of your youth . . . is your partner, the wife of your marriage covenant. Has not the LORD made them one? In flesh and spirit they are his. And why one? Because he was seeking a godly offspring. So guard yourself in your spirit, and do not break faith with the wife of your youth."[6] As far as God is concerned, marriage is far more than a mere social convention. It is a sacred commitment, the foundation of the home and of society. It is a divinely sanctioned state of oneness that can be paralleled only in the unity that exists in God himself. The divine rationale for this oneness was that "godly offspring" might be produced and subsequently nurtured in the admonition of the Lord.[7] Is it any wonder, then, that it has been asserted that marriage has always been the instrument of the survival of the Jewish people and of the preservation of its faith.[8]

God's design for marriage is inherently monogamous, with one man and one woman joined together first covenantally and then physically. This is clear from the first marriage. Polygamy is an aberration, a departure from God's design.[9] Though it is permitted because of infidelity, abuse, neglect, or hardness and infidelity of the human heart, divorce was never God's intention for his human creation. Jesus observed that "from the beginning it was not so,"[10] and he commanded that what God has joined together man should not put asunder.[11] Remarriage can also receive divine sanction in certain circumstances.[12] Neither divorce nor remarriage is preferred, however, because when they occur, God's original intent for human marriage in Eden has not been fulfilled.[13]

God's ideal must be the goal of every person and every marriage; however, the real condition of sinful humanity frequently falls short of the ideal. The reason that ancient Israel accepted divorce and remarriage was for the protection of the innocent victims of those who sinned against God and against covenanted married partners. Judaism's focus on social justice has been manifest first in society's most fundamental unit where the right to divorce and remarry has been upheld in situations of spousal abuse and neglect.

Dysfunctional individuals and families in the modern world are often the product of failure to follow God's instructions for human behavior. Men and women today, like their counterparts in all previous generations, have chosen to follow human perspectives on interpersonal relations rather than to be obedient to God's commandments. The result, as always, has been disastrous. It would profit all believers to review pagan concepts of marriage and compare them with biblical instructions to see which options more significantly influence their thinking and their lives.

In much of the ancient world, marriage was a mere social convention, a means of ensuring that a man could have some degree of certainty that his children and heirs were his own flesh and blood. In Greece and Rome, sexual and social pleasures were taken in the temples of the gods and in the company of prostitutes and courtesans, and such promiscuity was an accepted societal norm. In Greece, men kept their wives cloistered in the home, virtually under lock and key, because it was considered disgraceful for a wife to be seen in a public place unless she was in the company of her husband or of his designated chaperone. Men, on the other hand, had no such restraints. They could freely copulate with virtually anyone. As Demosthenes said, "Mistresses we keep for pleasure . . . wives are to bear us legitimate children."[14]

The predominant idea of love in these societies was based on eroticism. Men and women were always falling in love, victims of Cupid's arrows. This erotic kind of love, however, is not a sound basis for founding a home, for it is inherently selfish, borne out of the quest to satisfy individual desires for pleasure. This love lust is grounded in self-gratification and self-fulfillment. Partners, like Tristan and Isolde of Arthurian legend, are madly and hopelessly in love; however, their experience is really a mutual narcissism, a self-love of a passion-generated vision of the perfect lover.[15]

True love is an outworking of marriage. While physical attraction is important in this most intimate of relationships, as the Song of Songs clearly demonstrates,[16] marriages that are founded solely on erotic impulses are often doomed to failure because the sacrificing of the individual self-interest that is necessary in order to maintain and strengthen the greater whole is not their driving impulse. Usually, erotic lovers are more in love with themselves than they are with their partners and are focused more on fulfilling their own emotional needs and hormonal impulses than on satisfying the needs of their partners. The infatuation of "falling in love" is often based on the expectation of self-gratification and self-fulfillment, more on the desire to receive rather than to give.

Biblical marriage is based primarily on covenantal commitment to God and to one's spouse and only secondarily on love. The sages have suggested that this truth is illustrated in the fact that Isaac "took Rebekah, and she became his wife; and he loved her"[17]—and in that order. Only when it is nurtured in a close domestic setting can love become a permanent foundation for a home. Love is an essential ingredient for successful marriage, but it is true love, the kind that is considerate of the needs and desires of one's partner. It is a self-sacrificing love similar to that with which Christ loved the church.[18] This kind of love will focus attention on one's spouse, seeing that the partner's needs and desires are fulfilled. It confirms the view that the two are actually one and that pleasuring one's spouse is the foundation of pleasuring oneself. When both partners love one another unselfishly, both receive more than they give. True love produces satisfaction for the giver in the fulfillment of the spouse's needs and desires.

Marital love is not a platonic experience that has as its ideal an escape from physical contact and pleasure. Christian theologians through the centuries have postulated the idea that the "original sin" in Eden was sexual congress and that sin is propagated from generation to generation through the "concupiscence of sexual relations."[19] The ideal for much of Christianity, therefore, has been one of total abstinence from sexual intercourse either through celibacy or through overcoming the desire for physical intimacy in marriage except for the express purpose of procreation. Tertullian expressed clerical disdain for intimacy in marriage this way: "Between marriage and fornication there is a legal, but not an intrinsic difference."[20]

Sexual intercourse is a central element in biblical marriage. Whereas many Christian teachers have considered marital intercourse on Sunday to be sinful,[21] the Jewish understanding is that coital engagement on the Sabbath is a *mitzvah* (a good deed) and is blessed of God.[22] The truth is that God created both human genitalia and sexual desire, and his Word says that both were good.[23] Then he specifically commanded the physical joining of husband and wife in marriage so that those physical and emotional desires for intimacy would be fulfilled.[24]

As a Jewish teacher, Paul understood this biblically Hebraic truth. He declared: "But since there is so much immorality, each man should have his own wife, and each woman her own husband. The husband should fulfill his marital duty to his wife, and likewise the wife to her husband. The wife's body does not belong to her alone but also to her husband. In the same way, the husband's body does not belong to him alone but also to his wife. Do not deprive each other."[25] Though the subsequent church had much difficulty understanding and accepting it, the Apostle to the Gentiles readily understood this biblically Hebraic truth and accurately represented it.

Somehow the church has been ashamed to talk about what God was not ashamed to create. In its often smug self-righteousness and hyper-holiness, the church has often considered inherently evil and dirty what God called good at the moment of its creation. From a Hebraic perspective, all human organs are entirely neutral, and all can be used both for good or evil.[26] Anatomical parts serve various functions; however, none is evil *per se* or more inclined toward evil. Acts of intimacy in marriage, therefore, are far from evil. Indeed, they are blessed of God when they are carried out in mutual love and respect. The Scriptures command it: "Rejoice with the wife of your youth. Let her breasts satisfy thee at all times; and be thou ravished always with her love."[27]

Intercourse is the glue of biblical marriage. It is the literal fulfillment of the biblical commandment to "cleave" (be glued together).[28] While it also serves the physical function of procreation, its principal purpose is companionship and intimacy, bonding and renewing by entwined physical bodies the spiritual connectivity of the marriage covenant. This experience brings wholeness to both husband and wife, both of whom are designed by God to experience the ecstasy of orgasmic gratification.

Much of Christianity has propounded the myth of female asexuality. Indeed, until the twentieth century, the mere suggestion that a woman could have a desire for sexual fulfillment or could experience sexual pleasure would have been viewed as "casting vile aspersions on womankind."[29] Many have insisted that only women of depraved morality can experience either physical or emotional satisfaction from sexual intercourse. In this perverted thinking, they have argued that wives merely serve as receptacles for their husbands' passions. The biblically Hebraic truth is that God created female sexuality and empowered the female both physically and emotionally with the capacity for complete sexual gratification. As a matter of fact, in Jewish tradition a wife is encouraged to take the initiative in helping her husband fulfill her conjugal needs.[30]

From a biblically Hebraic perspective, not only is a wife expected to have sexual desires, but her husband is required to bring her sexual satisfaction. This idea is based on the commandment that prohibits a husband from going to war or engaging in any business for one year after marriage so that he may remain at home and "bring happiness" to his bride.[31] The Hebrew word translated "bring happiness" is שָׂמַח (samach) and has been interpreted by the sages of Israel to include a requirement that a husband bring his wife complete sexual gratification. In Jewish understanding sex is a wife's right and a husband's duty,[32] not vice versa as it has been perceived in much of the Gentile world. The Talmud declares that a man who "neglects his marital duties to his wife is a sinner,"[33] and it also teaches that a husband who ensures that his wife attains orgasm before he does is rewarded.[34] While any form of physical intimacy that brings pleasure to both husband and wife is acceptable,[35] sexual compulsion in any form that violates the conscience of either partner is condemned in Jewish law.[36]

The dynamic ideal of biblical marriage is one of mutual submission. Even the scriptural injunction for wives to submit to their husbands is prefaced by the command: "Submit yourselves one to another out of reverence for Christ."[37] Indeed, Paul's instruction, "Wives submit yourselves to your own husbands as unto the Lord," cannot be interpreted textually unless in the context of the previous verse, "Submit yourselves one to another," because the word *submit* does not appear in that verse (and is rather interpolated from the previous verse by the translators). What this text says is that marital partners exhibit mutual respect and deference to one another out of honor for the Messiah.

The superentity that married partners have formed through covenantal merger and fusion transcends their individuality. The oneness they have achieved supersedes everything that they could have been as individuals. Both husband and wife see this entity manifest in their life partner. When martial partners function together equally, with distinct (though equivalent and counterbalancing roles) the exponential effect can be truly godly; however, if the hubris of one partner is manifest in an attempt to dominate the other, the potentially divine effect is stultified, canceled, and silenced.[38]

Mutual submission means maintaining communication and receiving a mate's counsel. Abraham was commanded of God, "Listen to whatever Sarah tells you," when questions about Hagar and Ishmael arose.[39] It is through such acts of mutual support that the Jewish ideal of *shalom bayit* (peace in the home) is maintained. Creating and maintaining *shalom bayit* is viewed as a sacred trust and a holy task among the Jewish people. Daniel Maguire underscores this truth by saying that *shalom bayit* "is indeed a sacred concept, but it is the responsibility of both husband and wife."[40] For the husband, it is a divine instruction; for the wife, "the practices and values connected with *shalom bayit*" are seen as "the primary source for their devotion to God."[41] Peace in the home is the foundation of peace in the community and ultimately in the world.

Without the sanctity of marriage, there can never be sanctity in the home. The quality of family life can only be as good as the quality of marital harmony, and marital harmony can only be attained when each partner recognizes God first, spouse second, and self last. A solid, God-centered marriage that is grounded in biblical principles is the foundation of the family temple.

[1] Genesis 2:24.

[2] Mathew 19:6.

[3] Genesis 1:28.

[4] Erasmus, "In Praise of Marriage" in *Erasmus on Women*, ed. Erick Rumnell (Toronto: University of Toronto Press, 1996), p. 59.

[5] Exodus 20:14; Galatians 5:19. Adultery includes any extramarital act of sexual intercourse, whether heterosexual, homosexual, or zoophilic. Fornication involves any premarital act of sexual intercourse.

[6] Malachi 2:14-15.

[7] Ephesians 6:4.

[8] Ignaz Maybaum, "Tradition that Is Living" in *Marriage and the Jewish Tradition*, Stanley R. Brav, ed. (New York: Philosophical Library, 1951), pp. 54-55.

[9] In male-dominated societies, polygamy is almost universally manifest as polygyny, not polyandry. It seems that it is acceptable for men to have multiple wives but unacceptable for women to have multiple husbands! Islam's teaching and that of various indigenous societies is clearly in violation of God's original intent for marriage. Even the examples of polygyny in Hebrew history were not ordered by God, even though they may have been tolerated as a result of societal norms.

[10] Matthew 19:8.

[11] Matthew 19:6.

[12] Jesus decried the liberal view that permitted divorce for any reason; however, he said that divorce and remarriage are permitted in cases of marital infidelity (Matthew 19:9). Paul agreed that marital partners were free to divorce and remarry in cases of abandonment (1 Corinthians 7:15) and suggested that individuals should remain in the matrimonial state in which they came to faith in Jesus (1 Corinthians 7:27-31).

[13] Malachi 2:16.

[14] Demosthenes, *Against Neaera 122.*

[15] Jacob Weinstein, "Better Than Romantic Love" in *Marriage and the Jewish Tradition*,

Stanley R. Brav, ed. (New York: Philosophical Library, 1951), p. 205.

[16] For a complete discussion of biblical sanction of the physicality of love, see John D. Garr, *Feminine by Design: The God-Fashioned Woman* (Atlanta, GA: Golden Key Press, 2012), pp. 145-197.

[17] Genesis 24:67.

[18] Ephesians 5:25.

[19] Albert Henry Newman, *Manual of Church History* (Charleston, SC: BiblioLife, 1986), vol. 1, p. 366.

[20] Tertullian. *De exhortatione Castitatis*, ix.

[21] In the fifth century, Caesarius forbade sex on both Sundays and feast days, warning that children conceived on Sunday would be born either lepers, epileptics or demoniacs. See Dorothy Haines, *Sunday Observance and the Sunday Letter in Anglo-Saxon England* (Cambridge: D. S. Brewer, 2010), p. 11, n. 49.

[22] Hyim Shafner says that in Judaism, "sex between husband and wife is a *mitzvah*, but on Shabbat it is considered an especially holy *mitzvah*. It adds to the pleasure we are supposed to feel on the Shabbat, and the unity of two people mirrors the ultimate unity of God." See Hyim Shafner, *The Everything Jewish Wedding Book* (Avon, MA: Adams Media, 2009), p. 253.

[23] Genesis 1:31; Song of Songs 1:2.

[24] Genesis 2:24.

[25] 1 Corinthians 7:2-5, NIV.

[26] Michael Kaufman, *Love, Marriage, and Family in Jewish Law and Tradition* (Northvale, NJ: Jason Aronson, 1992), p. 119.

[27] Proverbs 5:18-19.

[28] Genesis 2:24.

[29] David M. Feldman, *Health and Medicine in the Jewish Tradition* (New York: Crossroads, 1987), p. 63.

[30] *Eruvin* 100b.

[31] Deuteronomy 24:5, NIV.

[32] Michael Kaufman, p. 227.

[33] Babylonian Talmud, *Yevamot* 62a.

[34] Babylonian Talmud, *Temurah* 17a; *Bava Batra* 10b; *Berachot* 60a.

[35] Maimonides, *Book of Holiness*, section 9.

[36] Michael Kaufman, p. 214.

[37] Ephesians 5:21.

[38] Charles Bryant-Abraham, "On the Restoration of Biblical Womanhood to the Christian Believer," unpublished paper, p. 3.

[39] Genesis 21:12.

[40] Daniel C. Maguire, Sa'diyya Shaikh, *Violence Against Women in Contemporary World Religions: Roots and Cures* (Berea, OH: The Pilgrim Press, 2007), p. 199.

[41] Maguire, p. 199.

Chapter 13

Men and the Family Temple

THE BLESSING AND KEEPING PRINCIPLE

So many diverse opinions on the role of men in the home and society have been projected in today's world that most men simply do not know what is expected of them or what to expect of themselves. From the chauvinism of the past, to the machismo of some cultures, to the chivalry of others, to demands for a unisex view of humanity—diverse ideas have been promoted for "true masculinity." Reacting to millennia of the abusive treatment of women in male-dominated societies, militant feminism has sought to redefine masculine roles. Some have projected the idea that women are superior to men, that all men are pigs, and that men serve only one function: the perpetuation of the species. Others suggest that men should somehow get in touch with their feminine side. With all of these diverse demands, men today don't know whether to flex their muscles or cry!

This confusion has produced a dilemma of self-identity and self-worth for many, if not most, males in today's society. While the situation has produced a healthy rethinking of male abuses in the past, the problem is that the reevaluation process has failed to return to the one source where accurate and work-

able information can be found about masculine roles. The Bible
has been viewed as either having contributed to the problem or
having been its outright source, not its solution. Differing ideas
of masculinity have been projected from a perceptive and reac-
tive basis rather than from an apperceptive and proactive stance.
Perceived evils of the past have brought reactions in the present.
This approach to historical problems, however, has often created equally destructive "solutions." What is needed is an apperceptive approach of purposely returning to the original models
to arrive at a healthy, productive understanding. Then, proactive
measures can be taken to restore those foundations,
contextualized for the diverse manifestations of society in the
world today. The answer is a return to the biblically Hebraic
models for manhood.

In most ways, men and women are alike, if not identical.
Genetically, less than one percent of human composition differs
between male and female. This should stress the absolute equality of men and women in their humanity and underscore the fact
that neither should dominate the other. There are, however, distinct differences, and these differences occur in very important
areas of life. The anatomical differences are obvious even to the
most strident of militant unisexists; however, there are also psychological, emotional, and spiritual differences. Differences, however, can only be projected as generalizations, not as absolutes
that can be applied in every individual. They are manifest in
categories of understanding and principles of application, none
of which is an absolute law to which there are no exceptions.

One of the roles of manhood was established in God's
declaration to the first man following the fall: "In the sweat of
your face you will eat bread."[1] It is specific, though not unique
to manhood that God has designated men to be providers. For
this reason, males tend to be more adventurous, self-assertive,
and competitive. They generally take more chances even from

childhood. Males tend to think more logically and clinically; therefore, in childhood they generally manifest greater interest in (and aptitude for) math and science skills than their female counterparts. Males also tend to be less in touch with their emotions and generally are less creative. Their thinking is essentially left-brain dominated, differing from females whose brain hemispheres are more directly connected so that they also think spatially and with block logic.

God's pronouncement regarding Adam was not a curse. It was a recognition that his post-fall role would continue the function that he had had from the beginning when he was commissioned to be a keeper of the garden.[2] The rigors would be expanded because of sin; however, the role remained the same. For this reason, males have always established much of their self-identity in their work. They define themselves and are defined by others on the basis of what they do. This is good in that inbred in man is a work ethic that promotes the survival and welfare of the human race. It can be bad, however, when men get out of balance with their work-defined self-image. Workaholic lifestyles can be debilitating to both men and their families.

Unlike women, men are not relationally defined; therefore, it is easy for them to be detached and clinical, giving little thought to the interpersonal interaction that is necessary for healthy families. For men, it is not "who you are," but "what you do." For this reason, males tend to be more ego-oriented than females. As a result, they need affirmation, not negation. They need a sense of worth; however, their self-worth is not measured by who they are, but by what they do. Men are by definition doers. It is a part of their role as providers.

An outworking of this role is the male tendency to "take charge," to rule. Indeed, in the beginning, humankind, both male and female, was given the right to rule over the rest of creation.[3] The Edenic ideal was for the man to serve as protector and provider and the woman to serve as a nurturer and balance to the man. Sin, however, has extrapolated those functions into a twisted form of co-dependency in which men have been abusively dominant and women have been pressured into submission beyond reason or divine intent. Spousal abuse has, therefore, generally been a male phenomenon, an outworking of sin in the most fundamental of human relationships.

There is, however, a need for someone to take charge, especially in times of impending danger. God has designed the male spirit to rise up and meet a challenge head on; however, he has balanced that tendency with the caution and care of the female personality. If this balance had not been in place, males would have destroyed the earth long ago with their reckless adventurism. Again, these generalizations are not absolutes, for there are men who are less driven, and there are women who are more bold and adventurous. The generalizations, however, reflect the divine intent in the way in which God structured male and female in every aspect of their existence.

The role of manhood in the family is clearly established in the first of the three blessings that comprise the Aaronic benediction. This tripartite blessing can be seen as coming from the Father, the Son, and the Holy Spirit. The first blessing is from the Father: "The LORD bless you and keep you."[4] It is uniquely the function of fatherhood, therefore, to "bless and keep." Blessing and keeping require men to reorder their natural instinct toward self-interest to think of others, specifically one's spouse and children.

Blessing and keeping also require work, man's defining activity. Without work, men have low self-esteem. Government programs that promote indolence and laziness are debilitating to men. Men who do not work are not fulfilling the most basic of instructions for masculinity: "In the sweat of your face you will eat bread."[5] They are not fulfilling their commission to bless and keep their families. Nothing could be more devastating to the male sense of self-worth than the failure to fulfill the responsibilities assigned to him by God.

Work becomes more than an exercise of toil and suffering when it is understood from a biblically Hebraic perspective. Work is worship, and every man's work is a ministry. These ideas sound entirely alien to traditional Christian understanding, for the church has projected the idea that only clergymen do "God's work," making all other labor purely secular and carnal.

The bifurcation of life into two hemispheres, the spiritual and the secular, has been one of the most debilitating devices that Satan has used against the health of the church and its fundamental unit, the family. As a result, some men's work has been demeaned while that of others has been elevated to a lofty status. Since their work has not been considered to be spiritual, most males have found very little of their self-identity in the spiritual matters of the church. They have viewed themselves in a secularist perspective, making it easier to escape responsibility for spiritual matters in their own homes and in the church. It has also set them up in opposition to the church's spiritual leaders, forcing them to vie with polished, professional "men of God" for attention and respect from their wives and children.

By removing the work that man is inherently driven to do from the neo-Platonic sphere of the material and secular and returning it to the realm of the spiritual as an act of worship, the biblically Hebraic understanding places work in the right context and elevates male self-worth to its God-given perspective. There is no difference of value between any work, for it is all spiritual, not carnal. Man's work is an act of obedience to God's command both in Eden[6] and in the Sinai proclamation: "Six days you shall work."[7] This view causes every man to understand that he has a ministry: the work to which God has called him. It also underscores to him the importance of maintaining spiritual standards in every aspect of his life, not just those few moments when he is "in church." Viewing his work as his ministry gives every man a sense of its importance in the eyes of God and places a weight of responsibility on his shoulders to do justice and love mercy in the marketplace and in the home.

The male composition is also defined in leadership. While not all men are leaders, the rule of thumb for masculinity has been a tendency to step up and take charge. This again is a God-given, innate characteristic that is essential for human well-being. The most important place for man to lead is in the home. This leading must be from a godly perspective of servant leadership. Otherwise, sin can transform God's good intention into a twisted and evil distortion of abusive relationships.

A godly man will take the initiative to lead his family in every aspect of life. His servant leadership will facilitate the physical, social, and psychological development of every family member. He will also lead by example, not by fiat. He will be lord of his home only because he conducts himself like the Lord of heaven by sacrificing his own needs and wants for the welfare of his family. Jesus set the example of familial love by giving himself for the church, his bride.[8] The Father demonstrated the same sacrificial love when he gave his only begotten Son to redeem his children, the human race, from their sins.[9] There is no sacrifice that is too great for men who are true servant leaders in godly homes.

The first sphere where husbands and fathers should lead their families is in social interaction. This is an area where most men need significant help because men tend not to be relational. They are usually laconic and are generally deficient in verbal expression when compared to women. Their conversation skills are often underdeveloped. First, most men suffer from an attention deficit syndrome: they just don't listen, and they don't want to linger in a conversation or discussion until understanding or clarification is achieved. Proof of this is seen in male domination of remote control devices and their ability to view multiple television programs simultaneously. Since women are more expressive, especially in verbal articulation, they have a biological need to talk, and they need someone to hear them, particularly their spouses. Women need to bring this balance of communication ability and attention to details to the home and help their husbands meet their own need for social interaction for the health of the family.

Leading in family social interaction takes commitment and time, both of which are often deficient in men. In order to lead, however, men must take the initiative and lead by example. They need to learn to listen creatively, to foster an environment in the home that is conducive to dialogue and communication. They need to learn to initiate the interaction if they are to be true servant leaders, standing out front and pointing the way through their own actions.

The second area where husbands and fathers should also lead is in study. Every Jewish father has the responsibility of leading his family in two areas of study. First, he must teach his children the Torah or the Word of God.[10] Second, he must teach his children a means of livelihood.[11] All successful homes must feature these two levels of teaching. Men must take the time to educate themselves in God's Word so that they can teach divine truths in the context of their families and not leave that responsibility to Sunday Schools and other church programs. Specific times must be allotted on the family calendar for just such educational efforts.

In order to "bless and keep" his family, a father must also either teach and mentor his children in job skills, or he must provide a plan of education that will inculcate those skills so that each child can have the knowledge and experience to be successful in the role and work to which he or she has been called. A wise father is one who recognizes early in a child's life the predispositions that the child has and then nurtures that child in the achievement of life ambitions.

Leading in teaching must be in the context of the ancient Hebraic model for the transfer of knowledge: "Come, walk the road with me." This was the methodology of the sages who understood that they taught better by example. As their disciples followed them down the road, they taught them from the life situations that they encountered. They conveyed understanding in what they did, so that their disciples imitated their lifestyle.

This is the very essence of Christian discipleship that must begin in the home. Jesus invited his disciples to follow him[12] and Paul encouraged believers to be followers of him as he followed Christ.[13] Learning is best acquired, therefore, by modeling the actions of leaders. Indeed, the Greek word Paul uses for "followers" is μιμητής (*mimetes*), which literally means "to imitate" and is the etymological derivation of the English words *mime* and *mimicry*.

In fact, this is what children do anyway. They imitate their parents, either for good or bad. Following in father's or mother's footsteps is perfectly natural for little children. Following in biblical times was a great honor. As a matter of fact, the greatest honor that one could have was to be covered in the dust of one's rabbi.[14] The dust acquired in sitting at the rabbi's feet or in following him along primitive roads and trails of ancient Israel was, however, only a physical demonstration of what had been acquired through the unique rabbinic learning process that Jesus himself, as an itinerant rabbi, employed. Likewise, children will always be covered with parents' dust. The question is, What kind of dust is it, dirt or gold dust?

The third and most important role that any father can fulfill in leadership in the home is that of leading the family in prayer and worship. This is perhaps the most neglected area of biblically

Hebraic manhood. Most Christian men have abdicated from this leadership role and, willingly or otherwise, have surrendered their responsibility to the church and its professional clergy. In order to "bless and keep," men must maintain the most important part of human life, relationship with the living God in their own homes. Prayer and praise, study and devotion—all of these lead to the development and preservation of a healthy, God-fearing home, with respectful, well-balanced, and maturing children.

Children learn faithfulness and integrity from the example of their parents, particularly their father. This begins the father's honor for the sanctity of the marital relationship. What was a requirement for leaders in the earliest church must be the ideal to which every man aspires. In order to be a Christian spiritual leader, a man must be "the husband of one wife." The Greek text of this passage is literally translated that the man of God is required to be "a one-woman man" (μιᾶς γυναικὸς ανδρἄ)—*mias gunaikos andra*.[15] This ideal of integrity is that each man must be wholly devoted to one woman, his wife. The same can be said of wives who should be completely dedicated to their husbands; however, the lesson of Scripture is focused on the man.

Jewish tradition suggests that women are inherently more spiritual than men; therefore, men need more discipline to live a godly life.[16] If this is true, then the primary responsibility for maintaining the integrity of the marriage that is the foundation of the family rests squarely on the husband's shoulders. There is no space in biblical faith for philandering or engaging in questionable dalliances with those who are not partners in the marriage. The ideal from the beginning was one man and one woman for life. Human failure has led to brokenness, which fortunately is not irreparable. God is definitely the God of mercy who restores and even heals what has been shattered by sin. He also provides opportunity for a second chance. Heartbreaking situations can be avoided, however, if partners in marriage are careful to follow biblical guidelines for their conduct and not allow themselves to be swept up in the worldly promotion of vain "happiness" promoted by emotional stimuli.

When men understand their God-given roles and learn the discipline of walking with God in fulfilling his instructions, they can live fulfilled, complete lives, lacking nothing. Maintaining the divine fatherhood principle of blessing and keeping and of teaching and leading is gratifying beyond any of the pleasures that hedonistic lifestyles can offer. The greatest legacy that a man can have is to have provided a godly home and to have reared God-fearing children.[17] When his children rise up and honor him as a man of God, he has his ultimate reward and satisfaction.

[1] Genesis 3:19.
[2] Genesis 2:15.
[3] Genesis 1:26-28.
[4] Numbers 6:24.
[5] Genesis 3:19.
[6] Genesis 3:19.
[7] Exodus 20:9.
[8] Ephesians 5:25.
[9] John 3:16.
[10] *Targum Haggai* 1:2 says that if a child "knows how to speak, his father teaches him the *Shema*, Torah, and the holy language; if not, it would have been better had he not come into the world." See Catherine Hezser, *Jewish Literacy in Roman Palestine* (Tübingen: J.C.B. Mohr, 2001), p. 49.
[11] Babylonian Talmud, *Kiddushin* 30b says that "a father is obligated to teach his son a skill," for "he who does not do so teaches him to steal." See Hayim Donin, *To Be a Jew: A Guide to Jewish Observance in Contemporary Life* (New York: Basic Books, 1972), p. 131.
[12] Matthew 4:19; 8:22; 9:9; 19:21.
[13] 1 Corinthians 11:1; 2 Thessalonians 3:7-9.
[14] *Mishnah, Perkei Avot* 1:4 says, "Let your home be a meeting place for the wise; dust yourself in the soil of their feet, and drink thirstily of their words."
[15] Sarah Tikvah Kornbluth and Doron Kornbluth, *Jewish Women Speak About Jewish Matters* (Southfield, MI: Targum Press, 2000), p. 26.
[16] 1 Timothy 3:2.
[17] Proverbs 23:24.

Chapter 14
Women and the Family Temple

THE NURTURING, PROTECTING PRINCIPLE

Throughout profane history and in most of ecclesiastical history, womanhood has been defined in categories that have little resemblance to the biblically Hebraic model. Confucius expressed the Eastern perspective on women when he observed that because "men must have mothers . . . women are a necessary evil."[1] For the Buddhist woman there are eighteen special hells, but if she lives virtuously through 1,500 rebirths she may be born as a boy and at last have the chance to reach *Nirvana* (nothingness).[2] Muslim women are trapped in an abusive system that legitimizes polygamy and serial divorce and sustains general abuse and domination of women by men.

The ancient Greek philosophers, on whose thinking Western civilization is founded, considered women to be inherently evil. Aristotle, the high priest of Greek rationalism, considered the female of every species, including humans, to be deformed males, physically, mentally, and emotionally, leading him to conclude that "there is no virtue in women."[3] Plato believed that if a man were sufficiently evil during his lifetime he would be reincarnated as a woman.[4] Following their political and philosophical leaders, Greek men were largely gynophobic and misogynistic.

Many philosophers preferred pederastic relations to heterosexual relations because they worshipped the male body. In their thinking women served only the function of procreation, and contact with them should be limited.

At the time of its initial move toward Hellenization and Latinization, the Christian church abandoned biblical roles for women and adopted models from Hellenic, Latin, and pagan cultures, most of which have been demeaning at best and downright diabolical at worst. Because it adopted its view of womanhood from Greek categories, the Gentilized church has considered women as inherently less spiritual and more susceptible to sin than men. Entrenched male ecclesiastical bureaucracies have imprisoned Christian women behind demands for silence and submission through a church doctrine and polity grounded in the prejudice and/or ignorance of self-serving leaders and "substantiated" by mistranslated, misinterpreted, and misapplied Holy Scripture.

During the twentieth century, Western women began to find release from their bondage to male domination through various political movements; however, the pendulum swung from one extreme to the other, forcing upon "liberated" women roles with which they have not been comfortable and removing from them roles and functions that they should have maintained. The result has been confusion and disillusionment in women and a significant diminishing of feminine self-worth in many areas. This should have come as no surprise, for when individuals take on roles for which they have not been designed or abandon roles for which they were designed by God, emotional chaos results.

Just as the church has presided over the emasculation of men, it has also been party to the disparagement, depreciation, and limitation of women. When early Greek and Latin church fathers sought to syncretize the philosophies of the Greeks with the Hebraic teaching of Jesus and the apostles, they succeeded in incorporating perverted Hellenic philosophical musings regarding women into the very doctrine and polity of the church. As a result, rather than being held in esteem as they were in ancient Hebraic culture, women have been viewed as second-class citizens of the kingdom of God. They have been characterized as being inferior to men in mental ability and spirituality.[5] Their fecundity and materialism have been viewed as curses and traps to draw men of God away from a truly spiritual life.[6] Demands for celibacy in the priesthood of the Western church were founded on these nonbiblical ideas.

It is exceedingly shameful that the "liberation" of women has occurred through secular and political pressures rather than through the leading of the church. If the church had maintained its Hebraic foundations, Christian women would never have been subjected to such deplorable conditions and status. Because it abandoned its biblically Hebraic matrix, the church was able to read into Holy Scripture the perverse ideas of the pagan cultures that they had been commissioned to liberate by the Gospel. Though some more liberal, socially sensitive movements in Christianity have been supportive of efforts toward the liberation of women, much of conservative Christianity has plodded along, clinging tenaciously to age-old, nonbiblical and even anti-biblical definitions of womanhood and feminine roles.

It is a wonder that the church has survived the pernicious ideas that have emasculated male believers and have imprisoned female believers in chains of bondage and submission. Needless to say, it is time for a revolution of restoration to occur in Christianity. The radical reformation of the sixteenth century needs to be taken to another level. Commitment to the Word of God rightly divided means commitment to interpreting Holy Scripture so that its intended meaning is understood, not a meaning that one wants to read into the text. It also means that Holy Scripture can be properly understood only when it is returned to the history and culture of the people who received it and to whom it first applied.

In order to understand proper roles for women today, the most ancient texts describing womanhood must be revisited. It helps to begin at the beginning. Biblical woman was not a divine afterthought, nor was she formed from male spare parts. She was never intended to be a part of male chattel, a possession to be bought and sold. She was never designed to be a servant forced to function in silence and submission. She was never inferior to man either physically, intellectually, psychologically, or spiritually. And none of these traditional views of woman-hood emerged as a result either Adam's or Eve's sin in the Garden of Eden.

When the biblically Hebraic mindset is brought to bear on the issue of feminine roles, some clear insights emerge. Woman was designed by God to be a perfect counterpart for man. She was not a different creation. She was a power equal to him,[7] lacking in nothing. The man and the woman were of the same flesh and blood, "bone of bone" and "flesh of flesh."[8] She was to be a partner in a mutually supportive relationship that would provide balance and well-being for both man and woman. The only difference between man and woman was one of function, of role. In Jewish understanding, while man provides physical strength and provision, the woman provides psychological strength and support.

Whereas man was to be provider through his work, woman was to be nurturer through her gift for relationship. Even a woman's anatomy clearly defines her role. She is equipped to nurture life in its most vulnerable stage. The womb around which God constructed woman is the safest place in the world for a human being for the first nine months of its existence. Subsequent to birth, the still helpless infant is nurtured at its mother's breasts, another clear difference between female and male physiologies.

Both of these anatomical features that are unique to womanhood have been elevated in Hebraic thinking to signify characteristics of God himself. In Hebrew, one of the words for divine mercy, רַחַם (*racham*),[9] is from the same root as the word for womb, רֶחֶם (*rechem*).[10] The extent of God's mercy is clearly manifest in the attention that a woman's body gives to a developing fetus. Likewise, women's breasts are paralleled in God's nature of providing sustenance to his helpless children. One of the significant names of God, *El Shaddai* (the Almighty), is connected with the Hebrew word for breast שַׁד (*shad*).[11] The very idea, then, that women are somehow inherently evil either because of their physiological features or their psychological orientation is perverse and should be banished forever from the language and the thinking of the church. Indeed, Christians would do well to adopt the Jewish understanding that women are inherently more spiritual than men because they better reflect the qualities of the Divine through their manifestations of protective, tender mercy and nurturing lovingkindness.

Women's role in nurturing is augmented by the fact that they are gifted in verbal expression, able to affirm and strengthen relationships. They are also far more in touch with their emotions than are their male counterparts.[12] Feminine hearts are more empathic, more easily touched with human suffering, and they generally manifest greater altruism than do males. This quality has been honored in the Jewish community and in the Hebraic heritage on which Jewish understanding was based. The ancient Greeks, on the other hand, associated excessive emotion entirely with women and even coined the word *hysteria* from the Greek word for womb, *hystera*. This was but a further manifestation of the dim view of womanhood held in Greek male society that valued rationalism and general absence of emotions above all. Even today medical definitions of hysteria assert that this psychological condition is "a nervous affection, *occurring almost exclusively in women,* in which the emotional and reflex excitability is exaggerated."[13] The stark difference in language between Hebrew and Greek could not illustrate more clearly the view of womanhood in the two cultures. The womb in Hebrew is connected with mercy. The womb in Greek is connected with hysteria.

Because the church incorporated Greek philosophical concepts of femininity into its doctrine and polity, it failed to realize the importance of feminine emotion to the health and well-being of marriage, home, and society. Because women were emotional, they were disqualified from important functions in church and society that demanded the "clear head" of male rationalism. As a result of this stance, the emotional qualities of womanhood have not been encouraged in the church and in some instances have been frowned upon and excoriated. The church has suffered a degree of impoverishment by not recognizing these qualities as a divine counterbalance to male perspectives in the home, in the church, and in society.

A woman is designed by God for nurture, but not just for nurturing children. She extends her nurturing nature in a protective stance toward her husband and her home. She was designed by God to support her husband in a sense that is parallel with that in which God helps his people.[14] She also possesses the divine gift for making a home, what has been called the nesting instinct. Woman seeks security in a protected environment for herself, for her husband, and for her children. More than mere instinct, this is a divine impartation of grace into the feminine spirit. The desire and ability to make a home are unique talents that God has given *sui generis* to womankind.[15]

In the Talmud, Rabbi Yossi suggested that for him the words *wife* and *home* are synonymous.[16] This underscores the fact that a woman's role as a homemaker is more than just the fulfillment of a biological urge. It is a God-inspired endowment, for the blessings she imparts to the home are more than biologi-cally driven; they are spiritual endowments as well. "A pious wife, living modestly within her domestic circle, is like the holy altar, an atoning power for the household," the sages of Israel declare.[17] Samson Raphael Hirsch made this observation on the feminine talent for homebuilding: "A whole combination of knowledge, insight, abilities, and skills as well as moral virtue and spiritual excellence make up the art of the home builder."[18]

Militant feminism has decried the "homemaker" role and has so equated homemaking with slavery that the modern, lib-erated woman has generally disassociated herself from this title. Home economics, once a course for girls in high schools, is now virtually nonexistent. Today's females want to be more than a homemaker. They've "come a long way, baby!"[19] The truth is, however, that those women who neglect their God-given femi-nine gift for creating and maintaining the safe haven of the home will only suffer present disillusionment and regrets in later life.[20]

A contemporary poster underscores the much-maligned homemaker's importance to the home, society, and the world. Titled "The Most Creative Job in the World," it says, "Taste, fashion, decorating, recreation, education, transportation, psy-chology, cuisine, design, literature, medicine, handicraft, art, hor-ticulture, economics, government, community relations, pediatrics, geriatrics, entertainment, maintenance, purchasing, di-rect mail, law, accounting, religion, energy, and management. Anyone who can handle all of those has to be somebody special. She is. She's a homemaker."[21]

While a woman's primary role of nurturer is manifest in the creation and maintenance of the home, roles for womanhood are in no way limited to the confines of the home. While the home should be a woman's priority, there are virtually no limits on the endeavors in which women can be engaged outside the home. Indeed, Jewish tradition suggests that a husband should encourage his wife to have interests outside the home. Husbands should invest their resources and personal energies in helping their wives find fulfillment both in the home and outside the home.

One need only look at the activities that brought honor to Solomon's Woman of Valor to see the many endeavors which a woman may undertake. This priceless wife of virtue was skilled in creating objects from fibers and cloth. She was in the importing business, acquiring food from far-flung places. She was skilled with cuisine production and serving. She was a real estate developer and a vintner. She was a successful businesswoman. She was a philanthropist. She was a wise and faithful teacher. She acquired wealth. In all, she was as successful outside the home as she was inside the family temple. Whatever she did outside the home, however, was done in the interest of making her home more secure.[22]

To determine roles appropriate for women in today's world, one need only look at those that they fulfilled in biblical times with God's approval and blessing. Miriam was a divinely gifted teacher (the definition of the scriptural word *prophetess*).[23] Sarah is said by the Jewish people to have been a greater prophetess than Abraham was a prophet.[24] Deborah was a judge in Israel, one of the highest leadership positions in the society of her time.[25] Esther was the queen of the world's most powerful nation in her time.[26]

This tradition that assigned women important roles in the community and in the exercise of religion in the Hebrew Scriptures was continued in the earliest Christian church. This was in complete continuity with the Hebraic tradition and in contradistinction to the Hellenic tradition that later infected and infested the church with anti-biblical postures toward women. Philip's daughters were teachers (prophetesses).[27] Priscilla was the more prominent teacher in a wife-and-husband team, demonstrated by the fact that her name is mentioned before Aquila's.[28] She was used by God to expound to Apollos, a "learned man with a thorough knowledge of the Scriptures . . . the way of God more perfectly."[29] Phoebe was a minister and patron of the Cenchrean church who was commissioned by Paul to transact church business in Rome.[30] Junia was an outstanding Christian apostle.[31] Women were leaders of house churches in early Christianity.[32] What can women now do in society and church? Whatever they did in Bible times with God's approval. It's that simple![33]

It is a great shame on the church of history and today that severe limitations have been imposed upon women both in societal and ecclesiastical roles because of the infiltration of Hellenism into the teachings and practices of the church. Instead of maintaining the pure faith of Jesus and the apostles that was solidly grounded in the Hebraic heritage of their ancestors, the Gentile church imported alien ideas into its doctrine and polity that have brought disillusionment to one-half of its constituency and unrealistic responsibility to its other half. Now is the time to go back to the Book and restore biblically Hebraic womanhood.

[1] W. Dallmann, *The Battle of the Bible with the "Bibles"* (St. Louis: Concordia, 1926), p. 36.

[2] Russell P. Prohl, *Woman in the Church* (Grand Rapids: Wm. B. Eerdmans Publishing Company, 1957), p. 50.

[3] Aristotle, *Generation of Animals*, 2.737a:27.

[4] Plato, *Timaeus*, 91a.

[5] Ruth A. Tucker and Walter F. Liefeld, *Daughters of the Chruch* (Grand Rapids, MI: Zondervan Publishing House, 1987), p. 130.

[6] Eric Jager, *The Tempter's Voice: Language and the Fall in Medieval Literature* (Ithaca, NY: Cornell University Press, 1993), p. 233.

[7] God's description of the woman he made was that of an *ezer kenegdo*, a Hebrew term that has been translated "qualified helper for [the man]." In reality, *ezer kenegdo* means "a power equal to him" and can be translated "an equal partner." See David Freedman, "Woman, a Power Equal to Man," *Biblical Archaeological Review*, 09:01 (Jan/Feb 1983), pp. 56-58. For a thorough discussion of this subject, see John D. Garr, *Coequal and Counterbalanced: God's Blueprint for Women and Men* (Atlanta, GA: Golden Key Press, 2012), pp. 135-155.

[8] Genesis 2:23.

[9] Genesis 43:14.

[10] Genesis 29:31.

[11] The majority of scholarship agrees that the word *Shaddai* comes from the Akkadian word for mountain, indicating God's sufficiency and strength (cf. David's statement in Psalm 121:1, "I will lift up mine eyes unto the hills, from whence cometh my help"). Some, however, have suggested that *Shaddai* is associated with the Hebrew word for breast, indicating God's complete sufficiency to nurture his children.

[12] Though from a Hebraic perspective men are free to express emotion, women are more in touch with and more expressive of their emotions. Though the quintessential Jewish men, King David and Jesus, both wept (1 Samuel 30:4; Psalm 6:6; John 11:35; Luke 19:41), it is a fact that women shed tears more easily than men.

[13] Emphasis added. The Hebrew word *ezer*, meaning "help," was used to describe the first woman in Genesis 2:18. This word does not connote inferiority of subordination, for precisely the same word is used to describe God: "God is our refuge and strength, a very present help (*ezer*) in time of trouble" (Psalm 46:1).

[14] For a comprehensive discussion of women's nurturing nature, see John D. Garr, *Feminine by Design: The God-Fashioned Woman* (Atlanta, GA: Golden Key Press, 2012), pp. 269-284.

[15] *Merriam Webster's Medical Dictionary*, quoted on the web page: http://dictionary.reference.com/search?q=hysteria.

[16] Babylonian Talmud, *Yoma* 2a.

[17] *Midrash Tanhuma, Yayishlah,* 6.

[18] Samson Hirsch, *The Wisdom of Mishle* (Jerusalem, Feldheim Press, 1966), p. 246.

[19] Slogan in a 1960s advertising campaign for Virginia Slims, the first cigarettes made expressly for women. Liberated women were free to inflict cancer on their bodies equally with men!

[20] Garr, *Feminine by Design*, pp. 300-301.

[21] Quoted in Michael Kaufman, p. 250.

[22] Proverbs 31:10-31.

[23] Exodus 15:20.

[24] *Exodus Rabbah* 1:1; Talmud, *Megillah* 14a. See Jill Hammer, *Sisters at Sinai: New Tales of Biblical Women* (Philadelphia: Jewish Publication Society, 2001), p. 252.

[25] Judges 4:4.

[26] Esther 2:17.

[27] Acts 21:8-9.

[28] Acts 18:18; Romans 16:3

[29] Acts 18:26.

[30] Romans 16:1.

[31] Romans 16:7.

[32] There were congregations in the house of Chloe (1 Corinthians 1:11), Lydia (Acts 16:40), Mark's mother (Acts 12:12), Nympha (Colossians 4:15), and Priscilla (1 Corinthians 16:19). John also wrote his second epistle to the "elect lady" (2 John 1:1). The term *elect lady* in Greek was *eklekta*, which likely indicated that this woman was an ordained (elected or appointed) minister.

[33] This is consistent with God's immutability. "I am the LORD, I change not," he declared in Malachi 3:6. "Jesus Christ the same, yesterday, and today, and forever" is a cardinal principle of divine immutability established in Hebrews 13:8. Anything that God has ever approved must in some form still be acceptable to him, including guidelines for human roles and behavior.

Chapter 15

Children and the Family Temple

THE HERITAGE OF THE LORD

The roles of children in society have changed rapidly and significantly in recent times, with various children's rights movements reacting to flagrant examples of child abuse with ever-increasing demands for children to be equal in rights and roles with adults. While child abuse is unthinkable in biblical categories, children are placed in a posture of protection and submission to their parents that does not confuse lines of authority and provides emotional and physical security that children need above all else.

In biblically Hebraic thinking, children are to be celebrated. "Children are a gift of the LORD. The fruit of the womb is a reward," the Scriptures declare.[1] When the very first human baby was born, his mother's reaction was, "I have acquired a man from the LORD."[2] The Bible even suggests that one who has many children is blessed.[3] Children are not a necessary evil or an unnecessary inconvenience. When conceived in the security of a believing family, children are considered to be holy unto God.[4]

Parents should be diligent to surround their children with love similar to the way in which the divine Father envelops his children in his love. Parents are responsible for providing love and security for their children, and, in turn, children are responsible for honoring their parents.[5] This is the basis for the second of familial relationships that follows the first relationship, marriage itself. While children are not joined together with parents in the oneness of marriage, they still share a sacred relationship that is akin to no other interpersonal human interaction. They are genetically, emotionally, and spiritually a composite of what their parents are.

Parents are responsible for teaching their children. As a matter of fact, the Hebrew word for parent, *horeh*, is closely related to the word for teacher, *moreh*, and both come from the root word *yarah*, an archery term that means "to hit the target." The word *Torah* also comes from this same root and means instruction (not "law" as it has been inadequately translated in most English versions of the Scriptures). The Torah is God's instruction for his children, his guidelines for successful living.

One of the specific reasons that Abraham was chosen to be God's blessing channel to all the families of the earth was the fact that God knew Abraham would "command his children and his household after him to keep the way of the LORD by doing righteousness and justice."[6] Likewise, God's commandment to Israel was that parents should teach his instructions "diligently to your children," and the first place in which this exercise of parental teaching was to be established was "when you sit in your home."[7] The home, then, has primacy in education and is the locus for spiritual and emotional maturation.

In ancient times, family teaching responsibilities began with the mother, who, according to Hebraic understanding, instructed infants until they were weaned.[8] A Jewish mother was "chiefly responsible for teaching her children the rituals and traditions of Judaism in the home."[9] The father was to the assume leadership in joining the mother to instruct the child until the child reached the age of puberty. Finally, beginning at the age of ten the child was to be educated by the teachers and rabbis in the traditions of Judaism. The teaching of children is so important in Jewish eyes that the sages said, "The world itself rests upon the breath of the children in the schoolhouse."[10] Scripture underscores the value of the instruction of both the mother and the father to their children by saying, "My son, heed the discipline of your father, and do not forsake [the law] of your mother . . . keep your father's commandment; do not forsake your mother's teaching."[11] A prime example of this homeschooling is Timothy, who was trained from infancy in the Scriptures by his mother Eunice and grandmother Lois.[12] Teaching, then, is a responsibility upon parents throughout their children's infancy, adolescence, and early adult life.

This instruction focuses both on the Word of God and on what has been termed "secular" education or learning to acquire job skills or a means of livelihood. This education may take place in formal schools; however, such institutions never relieve parental responsibility to be the primary educators of their children. Homeschooling is not, therefore, a supplementary training mechanism in Jewish life, both for spiritual and secular understanding. The home is the primary venue and vehicle for all education, and all other teaching entities are supplementary to family tutelage.

Both of these areas of instruction are designed to fulfill the biblical imperative: "Train up a child in the way he should go."[13] The emphasis in this passage is upon the way the *child* should go, not the way in which the *parent* would have the child go. The Jewish understanding of this instruction is that it is incumbent upon parents to discern what gift, vision, and ambition a child has and then to work at providing instruction that will help the child to excel in fulfilling that goal. Children will not necessarily have the same preferences and skills as their parents. Each child is different, and each one's individuality must be respected and encouraged. If God wanted children to be perfect replicas of their parents, he would have instituted cloning rather than childbirth. Parents who are wise, therefore, will not demand that their children live out parental fantasies but rather will encourage and equip them to pursue their own aspirations.

Parents must provide for their children. They must maintain the essentials of life: food, clothing, and shelter. They are responsible for maintaining a secure environment in which children can feel safe and loved. Wise parents will sacrifice their own pleasures for the health and welfare of their children, and they will be abundantly rewarded for having done so both in this life and in the world to come.

Part of the security that children need is maintained by parental discipline. Parents must establish definite boundaries for their children's conduct, and they must reinforce those boundaries continually. Children without borders are insecure, and their insecurity will manifest itself in various unsavory ways, both in childhood and in later life. Many parents are afraid to enforce conformity to family boundaries and rules for fear of alienating their children. "They won't love me," parents moan, excusing the permissiveness that is rooted in their inability to discipline themselves so they can, in turn, discipline their children.

In order to be effective, discipline must be immediate, definitive, and final. It must have the impact of the applied rod of historical discipline. Vacillation will create insecurity and demands for further leniency and will lead to eventual disillusionment and rebellion. Corporeal punishment is an available option that may be a final resort. Some in modern societies discount the value of physical punishment and even seek to bring the weight of the law against parents who employ it. The Bible, however, makes the option available. Solomon observed that "the rod of correction imparts wisdom, but a child left to himself disgraces his mother,"[14] and the wise man noted that "he who spares the rod hates his son, but he who loves him is careful to discipline him."[15] The ideal, however, is the use of other means of discipline with the same finality as corporeal punishment.[16]

In exercising discipline, however, parents should always remember biblical injunctions against being overbearing or vicious. "Fathers, do not provoke your children to anger, but bring them up in the discipline and instruction of the Lord."[17] Jewish sages teach that it is forbidden to be too exacting with children regarding a parent's honor. Instead, parents should be forgiving, even minimizing or overlooking children's mistakes whenever possible.[18] Christian parents should be careful to exercise the tender mercies and lovingkindness that the heavenly Father has demonstrated to them in passing over their sins and welcoming them into his parental embrace.

Children are required to honor their parents. One tenth of the Decalogue is devoted to this precept.[19] Honor for parents is just as important to societal well-being as prohibitions against murder and theft. Philo of Alexandria observed, "Who could be more truly called benefactors than parents in relation to their children? First, they have brought them out of non-existence . . . to nurture and later to educate, body and soul, so that they may have not only life, but a good life."[20] Honor is a lifelong filial responsibility toward parents.

Children may not always agree with their parents, nor are they required to do so. They are, however, required to *honor* their parents. This honor means obedience in childhood, and it means respect and care when they are adults and their parents are advanced in age. No one is permitted to circumvent his responsibility to honor his parents. Jesus himself excoriated those who sought to hide behind the temple as a means of avoiding their duty to respect and care for their aged parents.[21] Solomon declared that any man who "curses his father or mother, his lamp will be snuffed out in pitch darkness."[22] On the other hand, one who honors his parents is assured of long life in the first commandment with promise.[23] Paul summed up children's responsibility very succinctly: "Children, obey your parents in the Lord, for this is right."[24]

Children should be taught from a tender age the responsibility that they have to the family, to the community, and to the world at large. Innate selfishness must be addressed and removed from the child's psyche. One good way to accomplish this is to provide opportunities for children to give to others some of what is given to them. In Jewish homes, a *tzedakah* box is prominently displayed, and children are encouraged to place coins in the box to be given to those in society who are less fortunate. The box is termed *tzedakah* box (charity box) because in Jewish thought charity is connected directly with righteousness, which is the principal meaning of the Hebrew word צְדָקָה (*tzedakah*). Giving to the poor is an act of righteousness because it is done in obedience to God's commanded that one love his neighbor as himself[25] and that he give to the poor.[26] When a child comes to understand that he is not the center of the universe, that other family members have needs, and that one is responsible even to help those beyond the family circle, he is set on the path of *tikkun olam* (restoring the world).

Children also should be blessed on a regular basis in the security of the family temple. A host of biblical blessings is available to discriminating parents who understand the power of the Word of God and want to take on themselves the role of family priesthood that speaks God's benedictions into the lives of their children.

Children who are reared in the biblically Hebraic model for childhood will be set on a path toward relationship with God and will adopt strong family values that then will be passed on to the next generation. Biblically Hebraic childhood is a blessed state and an important part of the family temple.

[1] Psalm 127:3, NASB.

[2] Genesis 4:1.

[3] Psalm 127:4-5.

[4] 1 Corinthians 7:14.

[5] Exodus 20:12.

[6] Genesis 18:19, NASB.

[7] Deuteronomy 6:7.

[8] It should be noted that in ancient times infants were weaned at a much later age than in the modern Western world. In current Chassidic Jewish tradition, a boy's hair is cut, and he is taken by his father to his first day at school on his third birthday, signifying the transition from babyhood into childhood.

[9] Ina Taylor, *Judaism, with Jewish Moral Issues* (London: Nelson Thomes Ltd., 2001), p. 69.

[10] Jerusalem Talmud, *Shabbath* 11.9b.

[11] Proverbs 1:8; 6:20, *Tanakh* (Jewish Publication Society). The word *law* in brackets is a literal translation of the Hebrew *torah*.

[12] 2 Timothy 1:5; 3:15.

[13] Proverbs 22:6.

[14] Proverbs 29:15.

[15] Proverbs 13:24.

[16] Biblical instructions about corporeal punishment should be viewed in the light of the scriptural injunction that required "an eye for an eye and a tooth for a tooth." This *lex talionis* was to be interpreted and applied as a means of imposing fair monetary penalties for intentional or accidental injury, not a literal exacting of the commandment. Likewise, corporeal punishment should speak of the swiftness and finality of punishment and never be manifest as any form of child abuse.

[17] Ephesians 6:4, NASB.

[18] *Shulhan Aruch, Yoreh D'ah* 240:19.

[19] Exodus 20:12.

[20] Quoted in Michael Kaufman, p. 288.

[21] Mark 7:10-11.

[22] Proverbs 20:20, NIV.

[23] Exodus 20:12; Ephesians 6:2. Longevity is not guaranteed in response to honoring one's parents; however, it is a divine promise.

[24] Ephesians 6:1.

[25] Leviticus 19:18.

[26] Proverbs 19:7.

Chapter 16

Temples in Time

MAKING FAMILY APPOINTMENTS

The family temple functions in the same way in which sanctuary has always been designed by God to operate. It is created in time, not in space. Just as God never chose to create a physical structure in a geographical location somewhere in the universe and then demand that all worship directed toward him originate from that material structure, so the family should never attach its idea of sanctuary to a specific physical location.[1] The focus for the family must always be on the times that are set apart in order to create and maintain the quality of family interaction with God and with one another. The set-apart time, not the physical structure, is the temple.

In order to have a truly biblical family temple, one must be careful to avoid focusing energies on things that appear to promote family well-being but fail to provide enduring havens of secure, affirming relationships. Attractive alternatives to true sanctuary are many and varied, offering the unwary and undiscerning emphases that are foundations for disillusionment and eventual dissolution of the family. Counterfeits, no matter how attractive or imposing, can never substitute for the true family temple that God has chosen for the focus of his set-apart times and seasons.

SHRINES OF MATERIALISM

If one's notion of sanctuary is securely identified with a geographical location or with a physical structure, anything that disturbs that site or shrine or one's attachment to it disrupts, even destroys the sacredness of the space and its function. Families that make the mistake of attaching their identities to a house or to a certain social or even religious connection can find either the structure or the connection suddenly wrenched from them. Such a loss can be devastating, demolishing their corporate domestic identity and shattering their sacred interpersonal relationships.

Parents should be very careful to remember that success in life and the utopia of security they seek cannot be guaranteed by material assets, and they should be diligent to teach their children this foundational truth. In an age of glorified materialism and of the unrestrained quest for pleasure, one must be even more diligent to protect against societal imposition of the idea that success is measured by money, power, prestige, or fun. One perverse slogan of this self-possessed generation is, "The one who dies with the most stuff (or toys) wins!"

Ideas of sanctuary in space have produced the unthinkable. Fathers have murdered their entire families because their image of success was threatened. Mothers have killed their helpless infant children because their personal freedom and social connections were threatened by unwanted pregnancies. Children have slaughtered their parents in a blood-lust for instant fortune. Destroying one's most precious relations has been mistakenly viewed by a deluded few as the key to personal success and satisfaction.

At the same time, thousands more have resorted to less murderous means to achieve their ideas of security, engaging in deception, treachery, and perfidy that have astounded their families and friends. Levels of betrayal have been unthinkable. Children who have been nurtured on false demands for success in families consumed by materialism have sacrificed their familial relationships on the altar of the god *mammon* (unrighteous gain), and the consequences have been devastating to their families and to their own mental health. Self-imposed demands for instant gratification have caused many to descend into the abyss of hedonism's uttter debauchery.

Individualism's Insane Asylum

Postmodern Western culture has exalted individualism to an almost worshipped state. The result has been a generation that is intoxicated with the worship of self. Everything is to be sacrificed upon the altar of self-sufficiency, self-generated success. The attitude of far too many today parallels that of a particularly obnoxious politician when he arrogantly reminded nineteenth-century American newspaper editor Horace Greeley that he was a "self-made man." Greeley's reply to such hubris is still apropos today: "Thank Goodness, that relieves the Almighty of an awesome responsibility!"[2] Men who pursue their own agendas at the expense of corporate well-being often create history's greatest disasters. Their insane lust for power and success at any cost destroys both themselves and those around them.

The truth is that God did create human beings with free will that permits independent thinking and individual choice; however, God was not the author of egocentricity and megalomania in mankind. This is a learned trait that is not innate in the human personality as God designed and created it. It stems from the *yetzer ha-ra* (inclination toward evil) that according to rabbinic tradition is inherent in all humanity. The *yetzer ha-ra* involves the instinct for survival and self-preservation, which is good; however, when driven to extreme by Adam's sin and the sin of every subsequent human being, it can lead to selfishness

and incredible misanthropy.[3] Individuals who are taught by precept or example that fulfilling their own rights, wants, and desires supersedes the well-being of the corporate community of
which they are a part will inevitably find themselves imprisoned
in an asylum of selfishness.

The ideal of freedom is God's gift to all humanity. It is an
inalienable right of every human being. The divine gift, however, can become a curse if taken to the extreme that exalts a
person and demands that he have power, prestige, and perqui-
sites at the expense of his fellow man. Freedom is both an
individual and a corporate right. To remove or diminish either
is to destroy the ideal of freedom altogether. To exalt an individual right to the level that destroys the rights of the community is to invite autocracy, despotism, anarchy, and, ultimately,
societal disintegration. To exalt the corporate right so that it
destroys individual freedom is to invite the tyranny of forced
conformity to a uniformity that results in stagnation and death.

The answer to this dilemma is both familial and societal
promotion of both individual and corporate identity. This promotion begins in the home, where each child must be challenged
to personal achievement while at the same time being granted
the security of borders and limitations. Discerning parents will
recognize early on the inclinations and interests of each child,
and they will commit their energies to facilitating the child's
development toward success in that area. At the same time,
however, the parents must underscore the fact that each child is
part of a greater whole, first of the nuclear family,[4] then of the
extended family, and finally of society in general.

Children must be taught the ethic of ensuring that their
efforts toward self-fulfillment also work toward the betterment
of their families, their communities, and their societies. There
can be no true self-actualization[5] without the building of the
most fundamental unit of society, the family. The siren song of

the postmodern world, however, is stuck on one key: "me, me, me, me, me . . ."! In the face of all this extreme self-indulgence, the old maxim of yesteryear is still applicable today: "God first, others second, and self last." In today's self-indulgent world, such an idea seems patently absurd. Still, this formula works. Individual achievements must be weighed in the balance of societal contribution. People must be judged by how their accomplishments will contribute to the advancement, security, and well-being first of the family and then of humankind.

SACRIFICING SELF FOR COMMUNITY WELL-BEING

The necessity for balancing individual and corporate needs has long been understood by the Jewish community. As a matter of fact, it goes back to the first generations of the family of the Israelites who were the progenitors of the Jewish people. After generations of the assertion of individual rights and the resulting mayhem and murder that accompanied such demands, two siblings were able to subsume their own rights to the welfare of their corporate family. Manasseh and Ephraim were the first brothers who overcame the fratricidal carnage that had brought grief and division to the children of their ancestral families, like Cain and Abel and Jacob and Esau, and no doubt hundreds of others.

When their father Joseph brought these siblings to their grandfather Jacob for the most coveted patriarchal blessing, the head of the Israelite family crossed his hands so that the right hand of blessing rested upon Ephraim rather than upon the firstborn, Manasseh. Despite their father's insistence that he was making a mistake, Jacob continued the benediction that transferred the rights of primogenitor to Ephraim.[6] Manasseh could have reacted violently and sought to protect his birthright; however, both he and his brother learned to subject their own rights to the best interests of the family and community.

As a result of the attitude of deference that was manifest by these brothers, Jacob subsequently commanded that the transgenerational blessing that was to be pronounced by all Israelite fathers upon their sons should begin with these words: "May the LORD make you like Ephraim and Manasseh."[7] Far more illustrious names, including Abraham, Moses, David, and Samuel, could have been invoked upon the heads of the sons of Israel, but the names that are models for the conduct of Jewish males are Ephraim and Manasseh. The Jewish ideal is that one does have individual rights and aspirations but that one must also have the wisdom and fortitude to subject those rights and aspirations to what is in the best interest of the family and the community.

A Jewish man or woman thinks of self only in the context of community. How will one's action affect one's total family? How will it affect the nuclear and extended family? How will it affect the community? How will it affect the entire family of Israel? This mindset is inculcated from infancy in the consciousness of every Jewish child so that it becomes a maxim for both the individual and the corporate mindset. Each child is challenged to achieve, and the level of success is unlimited. Whatever one's chosen field of endeavor may be, the expectation is for excellence to be achieved. At the same time, however, the family and community are not sacrificed on the altar of the cult of self-worship. Wealth and power are not just means of self-aggrandizement. They serve the function of helping advance the well-being of one's entire family and community.

THINKING IN THE PLURAL

It should come as no surprise, then, that virtually all of the prayers of the Jewish community are offered in the first person plural. Some sages have even suggested that any prayer that is not offered in the name of the entire Jewish community is no prayer at all.[8] When one enlists God's intervention and support, it is not merely for self-indulgence or for self-accomplishment and security. It is for the blessing of the community. In Jewish thought, one must think of the community—of others—and not merely of himself when engaging in prayer to God.

Because he was a Jew, Jesus mirrored this Jewish mindset when he instructed his disciples in the proper way to pray: "*Our* Father . . . give *us* . . . forgive *us* . . . lead *us*. . . deliver *us*."[9] These immortal words of the "Lord's Prayer" were not an innovation; they were merely a synopsis of ancient synagogal prayers that predated the time of Jesus and were, indeed, the focus of his own personal and corporate prayer life.[10] Jesus even took the ideal of corporate responsibility to a level that was higher than that of his contemporaries in first-century Jewish society[11] by suggesting that the highest ideal was that one should lay down his own life for his family and community.[12] Then, he personally demonstrated the truth that he taught by sacrificing himself for the redemption of the human family from the bondage of sin and death.[13]

Jesus' own human will prompted him to seek to escape from suffering; however, as he prayed in the Garden of Gethsemane, he chose to subject himself and his own feelings to the will of his Father so that all men could come to repentance and receive the gift of eternal life.[14] He could have asserted his right to life because, unlike all men who had lived before him, he did not deserve to die because he had never sinned and was, therefore, not subject to the death penalty of sin.[15] He could rightly have demanded the sanctuary of his own safety, and he could have summoned thousands of angels to deliver him from pain and suffering.[16] Instead, like Manasseh of old, he recognized what was in the best interest of his family, the human family, so he freely sacrificed all his rights.[17] As a result, God has exalted him and has given him a name that is above every name.[18]

God's idea of sanctuary, then, is not in rugged individualism and personal accomplishment. One discovers the safest place in the world when he aligns himself with God's will to pursue the benefit and blessing of family and community. This is why Christians are commanded to love one another with the same degree of self-sacrificial devotion with which Jesus loved humanity.[19] True security is found in mutually submitted relationships totally free from the motive of self-aggrandizement.[20] True sanctuary is in familial community, and true worship begins in the context of the home with the family that fellowships, studies, and worships God together. When worship begins at home, it can be extended into a larger community—an extended family, as it were—where it can also flourish because it is built on the foundation of successful family worship.

TIME, THE ULTIMATE TEMPLE

In reality, the only true temple is one that is built in time. This is the one sanctuary that God himself built: a time capsule. He did so at the conclusion of his act of creation. The last thing that God made was a temple in time. After six days of creative activity, God set apart the seventh day for all eternity as time that is set apart for relationships. He created a time-temple, the Sabbath. The safety and sanctity of the home, therefore, are maintained by a temple in time.

Time is the one thing that one's enemies can never destroy. It is the one thing that cannot be eroded by elements or obliterated by nature's convulsive and cataclysmic upheavals. No matter what the physical situation, one can withdraw into a temple of time to worship the Creator and to be with family and community.

In reality, each person controls what he does with time. Tyrants can destroy temples, civic centers, and even homes; however, they cannot destroy time. Though imprisoned and tormented, human beings can set apart a temple in time.[21] This sanctuary costs nothing in terms of material resources. It costs everything, however, in terms of personal commitment to divine instruction. This temple in time demands ongoing, week-by-week renewal of the determination to give God and one's family the time that he, they, and one's self require.

This is why God set apart the Sabbath and blessed it. As a matter of fact, the Sabbath is the only immaterial thing that God ever blessed.[22] God recognized that the creation would need a sanctuary for repose, a medium for renewal and worship. It is for this reason that one-seventh of the divine genesis energy was expended on creating rest.[23] Perhaps this is because one of the most difficult things for men to do is to rest and enjoy God and family. As an answer to human restlessness and selfishness, God created the Sabbath. Indeed, God considered remembering his *Shabbat* to be so important that he devoted one-tenth of his thundering words at Mt. Sinai to the command: "Remember the Sabbath!"[24]

The sages of Israel observed that the text of Holy Scripture declares that God finished his work "on the seventh day."[25] What, they wondered, was the work that God finished on the seventh day since everything material was either created out of nothing or was formed during the first six days of creation? The only conceivable answer was that on the seventh day, God created rest or repose. The Hebrew word for rest is *manowach* which comes from *nuach*, the word that means "to stop." Similarly, the word *Shabbat* is from the root *shevet* which literally means "to sit down." The fundamental purpose of the Sabbath, then, is connected with the concept of cessation, stopping the routine work of life to rest with God and family. The idea behind the Sabbath is not entirely that of physical rest, even though such rest is a significant part of God's design for human beings and, therefore, is necessary for fulfilling the divine commandment to remember God's set-apart day. After all, God did say, "Six days you shall work, and on the seventh day you shall rest."[26] The underlying idea is that of cessation, stopping what one is doing and making time for rest and repose. God simply designed the creation in such a way that every seven days, it is best for everything to stop so time can be set apart for God and family.

To use a musical metaphor, there is always a need for a divine whole rest to be imposed on both the treble and bass clefs of life amidst the swelling crescendos of feverish notes struggling above the scale for success or amongst ominous tones plummeting below the staff into the depths of failure, defeat, and depression. Someone has suggested tongue-in-cheek that when Jesus invited his disciples to "come apart and rest,"[27] he really meant that if they did not rest they would come apart. The exegesis may not be sound, but the idea is! Human restlessness can be satisfied only by divine rest. And the divine rest that every human being craves begins with the set-apart times that wise parents reserve for blessing their families in their home-temples through fellowship, study, and worship.

MAKING APPOINTMENTS

More important than rest, however, is the time-temple that provides and promotes relationship with God and with family, both the immediate nuclear family and the corporate human family. With the Sabbath principle, once each week every family finds a retreat from the pressures of everyday life. Special time has to be set apart because the human tendency is to rush onward and upward, struggling to go where no one has gone before. Unbridled ambition almost never provides for cessation. It is only when one fully recognizes the importance of temporal sanctuary that he will make provision for its establishment and maintenance. As Abraham Joshua Heschel said, "Some religions build greatcathedrals or temples, but Judaism constructs the Sabbath as an architechture of time. Creating holiness in time requires a different sensibility than building a cathedral in space: 'We must conquer space in order to sanctify time.'"[28]

In the Jewish celebration of *Shabbat*, time is made for everyone. First, a divine appointment is kept because *Shabbat* is the first of God's *mo'edim* (appointments) that are outlined in Leviticus 23.[29] God himself has made this appointment on his calendar so he can meet with his family. When God's children match this divine appointment with set-apart time on their calendars, a miracle of spiritual renewal and physical regeneration takes place.

This is why God made time management one of his ten preeminent instructions for the human race. "Remember the Sabbath to keep it holy,"[30] he commanded. God realized from the moment of humanity's creation that time management was as important to human well-being as as avoiding murder, theft, and adultery. Humans do not usually recognize that more can be accomplished in six blessed days than in seven unblessed days. This is why God blessed the Sabbath—so that it would be a blessing. When one sets apart one-seventh of his time for God and family, renewal is inevitable. Then, the works of his hands are blessed. The same is true for money, the counterpart of time. More can be accomplished with 90 percent of blessed money than with 100 percent of unblessed money. With time, one-seventh is God's; with money, one-tenth belongs to him.

Rest for rest's sake, however, is not the fullness of the Sabbath. Its essence is the building and nurturing of relationships. First, one renews and strengthens relationships with the Creator, understanding and confirming that existence and sustenance are not self-generated but are the result of divine providence. God is man's source; therefore, the believer does not hesitate to follow God's instruction to cease from labors for livelihood and rest in God's provision. Setting apart one day out

of seven specifically for the purpose of worship in a holy con-
vocation prescribed by divine appointment confirms and strengthens a person's vertical relationship with God.

At the same time, however, the Sabbath is no more restricted to worship directed toward God than it is restricted to
total cessation from any physical activity. Sabbath is also time
for family. Many Christians have missed this important truth and
have preoccupied themselves with the work of rest and worship
on their Sabbath and have, consequently, found themselves ex-
hausted at its end. They have worked so hard at *keeping* the
Sabbath that they have failed to *delight* in the Sabbath, God's
temple in time. The Sabbath is not a constraint upon one's time:
it is a delight, a liberating joy.[31] Jesus well observed that it is
lawful to do good on the Sabbath day.[32]

Because the Jewish people have been the longest and most
faithful celebrants of God's Sabbath, they have discovered the
enriching experience of the true temple in time. The focus of
the Jewish *Shabbat* is on the family, first the nuclear family and
then the extended corporate family. For Jewish families, the
Sabbath, therefore, begins in the home. Father, mother, and
children retreat from the hustle and bustle of everyday life into
the sanctuary of the Sabbath and even invite guests to join them
in their family temple that has assembled in time.

As the sun sets on Friday evening, the Jewish family leaves
the challenges of ordinary life and enters its temple, the Sabbath. The door to the frenetic activity of life is closed, shutting
out the ordinary, opening up the divine. As the mother lights
candles welcoming both the Sabbath and God's presence into
their home, the family temple of safety, security, and peace is
reconstituted and reaffirmed so that in the Jewish home each
family member basks in the warm glow of affirmation and blessing.

Why does such a high level of solidarity exist in Jewish
families and in the Jewish community in general? The answer is

that family bonding occurs on a regularly scheduled basis. Sabbath offers a weekly opportunity to renew and strengthen family relationships and to underscore relationality with the living God in the context of the family and community. The synagogue experience is not a performance-based, audience-based exercise that preserves anonymity as is the case with many Christian corporate worship experiences. Instead, it is highly participative. It reaffirms relationships between family members and strengthens their connection with the larger Jewish community.

The Jewish family and the Jewish community, then, are blessed because they spend one-seventh of their time in their time temple, cloistered from the pressures of the world about them, basking in loving, supportive relationships, and thinking of their blessedness as God's chosen people. Because they have engaged one another and God in the intimacy of their homes, congregational gatherings are celebrations of life and the opportunity to worship God together as an extended family and community.

God's Appointments with His Family

Because humans are inherently forgetful and because they become so caught up in the routines of life that demand more and more of their time, God has devised a system of remembrance to deal with the universal problem of human forgetfulness. The divine principle that requires remembrance is codified in the first word of the fourth of God's Ten Commandments: "Remember!" This divine imperative is one of ten categories of commandments that are essential for walking with God by following his instructions for successful living.

The specific remembrance that is commanded in this instruction is to set apart the Sabbath as a memorial of creation (the general command for all humanity)[33] and as a memorial of deliverance from Egyptian bondage (the specific command for the Jewish people).[34] God's Sabbath command speaks to the

Jewish heart that it is important to remember that God delivered them from the seven-day-a-week enslaving work of the Egyptian taskmasters. The Sabbath command still speaks to the non-Jewish heart reminding the believer that God—and God alone—created the heavens and the earth and everything in them and that he sustains everything that he has created.

Setting apart one day in seven as a time devoted entirely to God and to family is vital to human health and to human spiritual welfare; however, it is only part of God's remembrance plan. God's calendar includes daily, weekly, monthly, seasonal, and generational appointments that he has made for meeting with his children. Scripture has always underscored the fact that time must be planned, scheduled, and set apart for family; therefore, it has made provision for a systematic outline for "time out" from life's routine that provides opportunity for the single most important things in human existence: relationships. Because interpersonal relationship is both vertical and horizontal, God's design is for time to be spent in communion first with him, then with family and community. The only way to ensure that this would occur was for God to establish set times.[35]

First, God established daily hours of prayer. These set times for God to meet with his children are morning, noon, and evening. In antiquity, they were 9 a.m., noon, and 3 p.m. The morning and afternoon hours of prayer coincided with the required times of sacrifice in the tabernacle and temple.[36] King David observed the three hours of prayer, saying that he was faithful to pray "evening, morning, and at noon."[37] Centuries later, these were the same three times a day when the prophet Daniel prayed in Babylon with his window open toward Jerusalem.[38] His absolute and unequivocal determination to meet God's daily prayer appointments landed him in the king's den of lions, but it also brought about his miraculous deliverance.

The tradition of praying three times a day continued among

the Jewish people and was a prominent aspect of the daily lives
of Jesus and the apostles. As a matter of fact, the only place in
the Bible where the term *hour of prayer* is specifically mentioned
is Acts 3:1 where it describes an event in the days of earliest
Christianity. A cursory review of the apostolic era, however,
reveals continuing compliance with the outline for daily prayer
that David and Daniel practiced. Jesus was crucified at 9 a.m.,
the morning hour of prayer,[39] darkness covered Jerusalem at the
noon hour of prayer,[40] and Jesus expired at 3 p.m., the afternoon
hour of prayer.[41] The Holy Spirit was given to the church on the
day of Pentecost at the morning hour of prayer.[42] Peter was
praying on the housetop at the noon hour of prayer[43] when he
received the commission to take the gospel to the household of
Cornelius, the Roman centurion had been visited by the angel
during the afternoon hour of prayer of the previous day.[44] Paul
received his divine visitation on the Damascus road at the noon
hour of prayer.[45] The lives of the earliest Christian believers
were punctuated daily by the hours of prayer.

Throughout their history, the Jewish people have continued
to honor the hours of prayer. To this day, they remain faithful
to the ancient biblical formula, praying three times a day: *Shacharit*
(in the morning), *Mincha* (in the afternoon), and *Ma'ariv* (in the
evening). The daily prayer appointments that God established
on his calendar for meeting with his children have been much
valued throughout salvation history, and they continue to be
important in the Jewish community. Christians, too, can share in
this prophetic and apostolic practice, thereby fulfilling Paul's
instructions that they "pray without ceasing."[46] Believers who
propose to walk daily in the presence of God will welcome and
apply the divine principle of remembrance that establishes three
set times for prayer each day in the family temple.

God's weekly divine appointment is *Shabbat*. Many have
suggested that Paul's instructions in Romans 14:5 suspended the

responsibility for Sabbath remembrance from all believers, particularly Gentiles. While it is true that no one's salvation or relationship with God can be judged by the days he observes or does not observe or by the manner in which he observes them,[47] it is also true that God's instruction regarding *Shabbat* has never been abrogated. We have Jesus' personal word on it! "Think not that I have come to destroy the law or the prophets. I have not come to destroy but to fulfill,"[48] he declared. Making every day exactly the same (as some have interpreted the Romans text) has produced a kind of pansabbathism, which in effect is to have no Sabbath at all. If every day is the Sabbath, then no day is the Sabbath. Instead of spending endless amounts of energy trying to explain away God's instructions, believers would be better served by simply adopting Israel's reaction to the divine wisdom, "Whatever you have said, we will do,"[49] and begin to set apart one day in seven for God and family.

Israel also has a monthly appointment with God called *rosh kodesh*, the new moon.[50] This is another time to stop and consider that God is the author of everything including time. For believers, the first of each lunar cycle would be a good opportunity to evaluate their walk with God during the previous month and to make plans and commitments for the next month. If monthly reevaluation is good for business, how much more is it healthy for the family. This is far better than New Year's resolutions that can be forgotten within weeks only to be dusted off and guiltily reaffirmed a year later.

God's chosen people were also given three major seasonal appointments that were expanded into seven and finally into nine. God's three festivals are Passover, Pentecost, and Tabernacles.[51] Ancillary to these are Unleavened Bread and Firstfruits (around the time of Passover)[52] and Trumpets and the Day of Atonement (near the time of Tabernacles).[53] Later, the Jewish people added Purim to celebrate their victory over a genocidal attempt against them in the days of Queen Esther. Then, they began to observe Hanukkah to memorialize their victory over a vicious effort to destroy Judaism through assimilation into Hellenism during the time of the Maccabees. The biblical festivals are specifically called *mo'edim* (appointments) in the Hebrew Scriptures[54] and are, therefore, scheduled meetings between God and his children.

Finally, God made generational appointments with his people, including the Sabbath year, called the *shmita*, because its most prominent feature was the year of "release" (the meaning of *shmita*). This was the time when once every seven years all things are returned to their natural state, and the land of Israel was permitted to rest by not being tilled.[55] Additionally, there was also a Year of Jubilee that occurred every 50 years (seven Sabbath years plus one year).[56] This was the great year of release when all debts were paid and everyone in society was returned to a state of economic equilibrium.

God's calendar, then, provides for a series of appointments that impact all of human life. The wise will consider God's instruction to "remember" by employing the divine calendar to meet with God, with family, and with community. Wisdom would suggest that rather than devise one's own calendar, it would be more practical and efficient simply to adopt and utilize God's appointment calendar. If that calendar was good enough for Jesus and the apostles, surely all believers would welcome it and make it their own specifically designated biblical times set apart daily, weekly, monthly, seasonally, and generationally. When they do so, a virtual symphony of family interaction can build the euphony family solidarity and dedication to God.

FAMILY APPOINTMENTS

If God thought it was important to establish set times of remembrance to meet with his children, how much more should Christian parents understand the need to make appointments with one another, with their children, and with their extended families and communities. Making time is essential to health and happiness. Those who fail to make appointments end up lamenting their loss in the words of the popular song, "Ain't it funny how time slips away?"[57] Those who follow God's leadership by making daily, weekly, seasonal, and generational appointments to meet with God, with family, and with community find that spiritual growth and healthy interpersonal social relationships result.

Just as God has made appointments on his calendar, however, man must also establish set times for himself and his family. Time must be made for God and family. Otherwise, it will be consumed by self-absorbed, time-depleting human nature. One wakes up too late to wonder, "Where did all the time go?" The Romans recognized the fleeting nature of time in their oft-repeated maxim, "*Tempus fugit*" ("time flees" or "time flies"). The Latin poet Virgil expressed this truth and its consequences very succinctly: "*Sed fugit interea fugit irreparabile tempus, singula dum capti circumvectamur amore*," meaning, "But meanwhile it flees: time flees irretrievably, while we wander around, prisoners of our love of detail."[58] Succinct, indeed! Human beings are almost always so caught up wandering around obsessed with details of life that they neglect the important things and then wonder where all the time went. The fleeting and limited time that one has is far too often consumed by things with little or no intrinsic substance. Unless one makes a conscious and concerted effort to sanctify time, it will all become a blur, with one moment becoming indistinguishable from next and, in the end, all seemingly wasted in vanity.

First, every family should establish set times daily for family interaction. The specific hour is not nearly as important as the fact that times are set. Schedules vary from family to family; therefore, what is most convenient should be adopted. Exacted, punctilious observance is not as vital as fulfilling divine principles. The important thing is to establish specific daily times for family, preferably morning, noon, and evening, but at least at morning and evening, the timing of the daily temple sacrifices. If done on a consistent basis, the exercise need not be laborious or drawn out unnecessarily. A simple, short Bible reading, a prayer, and a social exchange between spouses and between parents and children will become a much-anticipated event. This can easily be done in the morning before work and school, at noon before lunch, and in the evening at dinner or before bed-time. If everyone can stop and take time to eat breakfast, lunch, and dinner, surely they can take time to pray even a short prayer three times a day. If set times are established each day, fathers will make more time for communicating with their children. Growth will occur, and family solidarity and unity will ensue.

In addition to daily appointments for the entire family, parents must establish set times for their own personal interaction. Children must be made to understand that father and mother are also husband and wife and that their relationship must also be nurtured with set times. A locked bedroom door establishes the fact that there is an intimacy between father and mother that is different from other family relationships. It establishes an inner sanctum in the family temple and confirms to spouses that their intimacy is so valued as to be nurtured in the time sanctuary of appointments made specifically for one another.

Second, weekly times must be set apart for family and God. *Shabbat* is a good time for this interaction, a time for family fellowship, study, worship, and blessing. If Friday evening is inconvenient for the family, another time can be substituted; however, working toward making time that corresponds with God's calendar is a good idea. During this weekly family day, heads of household should assume God-given roles of priesthood to lead families in things pertaining to one another and to God.

Third, it would be very helpful for each family to meet together around the first of each month to review their progress, to see how they have done in maintaining family unity and keeping their family temple secure and strong. Each family can choose when and how to do this. Time and method of observance can be very fluid, designed to meet the need of each individual family. What is important is that everyone stops periodically to remember, to reevaluate, and to renew, thereby fulfilling the biblical principle.

Fourth, seasonal appointments can be made that underscore family solidarity by remembering salvation history, studying God's Word, and worshipping together as a family unit. God's festivals not only have family significance and application, their observance was designed first for family and only then in the context of community. Passover, Pentecost, Tabernacles and other festivals of biblical tradition can be much-anticipated yearly exercises that bring family and friends together for special times of celebration that are more than the usual weekly events.

Generational appointments can be wide and varied. Besides a Year of Jubilee celebration, various rites of passage in family life can be generational appointments to share quality time with one another and with God. These can include confirmations or *bar/bat mitzvahs* at the time when children reach puberty. They can be graduations, weddings, wedding anniversaries, family reunions, and other important family events. Again, the important thing is not the specific event but that appointments are made and kept.

TIME MANAGEMENT

Establishing and maintaining family appointments takes work. If no one is diligent to insist that the appointments are kept, they will degenerate to the point that they will be nonfunctional and meaningless. The second law of thermodynamics, called the law of entropy, establishes the scientific fact that anything left to itself without the constant intervention by an outside force will become less ordered and will degenerate into a state of inert uniformity. Somebody has to do something to set the action in motion, and someone has to do something to maintain its operation. There is no such phenomenon as perpetual motion. For every effect, there must be a cause. Spouses must, therefore, act to establish and maintain set times before their union is blessed with children. Then, they must keep their appointments and see that their children remember them as well.

Time is not an enemy if one sets apart what God has requested. Appointments are established as a divine principle. Those who propose to engage in *imitatio Dei* or who seek to be truly *Christian* will follow the Father's example by setting and maintaining appointments for God and family. In so doing, the family sanctuary will be a temple in time where materialism matters little and relationship is everything! In an era when virtually everyone has a smartphone, a laptop, or a tablet to manage time and remind them of important business appointments, how much more should Christians have a predetermined calendar that reminds them of the most important things that they have in their lives, the times that they spend with God and their families. To do otherwise is to invite chaos, for those who do not plan and manage time will be consumed by the demands of time that will simply overwhelm them and make it virtually impossible to have spontaneous, quality family time. They will only react to the disasters and problems of life that will inevitably come. This is because average people wait and react. Successful people, on the other hand, plan and act. If believers will plan and manage their time like God does, they will discover that it is not as difficult as they thought to build a temple in time, a dimension of fellowship, study, and worship that strengthens the bonds of relationship both with God, with family, and with community in the family temple.

[1] The material sanctuary that God commanded was the tabernacle, a portable structure that accompanied the people. The temple that became the focus of Judaism during the monarchy and afterward was constructed because of King David's passion to build a sanctuary for God. Jesus declared that the ideal for worship was not in any mountain, including the temple mount, but in spiritual truth manifest in human hearts (cf. John 4:21-23).

[2] Horace Greeley, quoted in Insults.net at the website: http://www.insults.net/html/behaviour/arrogance.html

[3] Rabbinic thought suggests that there are two inclinations in each human being, an inclination toward good (*yetzer ha-tov*) and an inclination toward evil (*yetzer ha-ra*). Even the evil inclination has a good element in that it involves survival instincts; however, if not controlled by the inclination toward good, even these elements necessary for human existence can become perverted and used by Satan to foment incredible evil in the world. The conflict between the two *yetzers* in every human heart is the battle in the mind described by Paul in Romans 7:16-20 and 2 Corinthians 10:5. It is the spiritual warfare in which every believer engages.

[4] The "nuclear" family is comprised of father, mother, and children.

[5] The term *self-actualization* was introduced by organismic theorist Kurt Goldstein to describe the human motivation to realize his full potential (Kurt Goldstein, quoted in Arnold H. Modell, *The Private Self* [Cambridge, MA: Harvard University Press, 1993], p. 44). The term was brought popularity when psychologist Abraham Maslow made it the highest part of his hierarchy of needs (Ricky W. Griffin and Gregory Moorhead, *Organizational Behavior: Managing People and Organizations* [Mason, OH: South-Western CENGAGE Learning, 2010], p. 93.

[6] Genesis 48:14.

[7] Genesis 48:20.

[8] Babylonian Talmud, *Berachot* 29b-30a. See Hayim H. Donin, *To Pray as a Jew: A Guide to the Prayer Book and the Synagogue Service* (Jerusalem: Moreshet Publishing, 1980), p. 359.

[9] Matthew 6:9-13.

[10] Edward Kessler, *An Introduction to Jewish-Christian Relations* (Cambridge: Cambridge University Press, 2010), p. 17. Kessler points out, "The prayer begins with the main concerns of the *Kaddish* and then follows the outline of the *Amidah* (Eighteen Benedictions): praise, petition and thanksgiving. The hallowing of God's name is an essential part of both the Lord's Prayer and the *Kaddish*, as it refers to the coming of God's kingdom." He also references David de Sola Pool who wrote that the Lord's Prayer has an "exact equivalent in the *Kaddish* [prayer of mourning], except for differences in person."

[11] It is generally understood in Jewish thought that one is responsible for preserving life in danger, but he is not required to sacrifice his own life in order to save the life of another. This is based on the Jewish view of the sanctity of all human life. The sages ruled that while a man "had no right to save his life by causing the death of another," at the same time, "he was not required to sacrifice his life to save another." See Paul Johnson, *History of the Jews* (New York: Harper & Row, 1987), p. 155.

[12] John 15:13.

[13] Hebrews 2:14-15.

[14] Luke 22:42.

[15] Romans 6:23; 2 Corinthians 5:21.

[16] Matthew 26:52-54.

[17] Genesis 48:14; Philippians 2:6-8.

[18] Philippians 2:9-10.

[19] John 13:34.

[20] Ephesians 5:21.

[21] A prime example of a time-temple was that of Paul and Silas who were incarcerated in a Roman jail but chose to turn their prison into a temple for the worship of God (Acts 16:25). As a result of their actions, a profound miracle occurred when the prison was shaken by an earthquake and they were freed from their bonds.

[22] Exodus 20:11.

[23] Genesis 2:2.

[24] Exodus 20:8.

[25] Genesis 2:2.

[26] Exodus 23:12.

[27] Mark 6:31.

[28] Abraham Joshua Hechel, *The Sabbath* (New York: Farrar, Strauss, and Giroux, 1951), p. xiii. The idea of a sanctuary in time rather than in space is founded on the principle established by Heschel, While the principle is anchored in the Sabbath, it also extends to other set times for family and God which that are discussed here.

[29] Leviticus 23:2-3.

[30] Exodus 20:8.

[31] Isaiah 58:13.

[32] Matthew 12:9-12; Mark 3:1-4.

[33] Two delineations of the Ten Commandments are given in Scripture. The first enjoins Sabbath observance because "God created the universe in six days and rested on the seventh day" (Exodus 20:8-11). This version, the command to remember weekly that God—not nature or some other force or happenstance—is the creator of everything that exists is incumbent upon all humanity. This commandment was universal because its "therefore" was related to the creation in six days and the rest on the seventh day.

[34] The second delineation of the Ten Commandments says of the Sabbath in Deuteronomy 5:12, 15, "Observe the Sabbath day by keeping it holy. . . . You shall remember that you were a slave in the land of Egypt, and the LORD God brought you out of there by a mighty hand and by an outstretched arm; therefore the LORD your God commanded you to observe the sabbath day." This commandment was specific to Israel because its "therefore" was related to Israel's slavery in Egypt.

[35] The biblical festivals were called *mo'edim*, which means "set times."

[36] Leviticus 9:17 speaks of the "morning sacrifice" (*alah boker* in Hebrew). 2 Kings 16:15 speaks of the "evening grain offering" (*olah minchah* in Hebrew). (Daniel 9:21 speaks of the "evening offering" (*erev minchah* in Hebrew).

[37] Psalm 55:17.

[38] Daniel 6:10-13.

[39] Mark 15:25.

[40] Mark 15:33.

[41] Matthew 27:46.

[42] Acts 2:15.

[43] Acts 10:9.

[44] Acts 10:3.

[45] Acts 22:6.

[46] 1 Thessalonians 5:17.

[47] Colossians 2:16.

[48] Matthew 5:17.

[49] Exodus 24:7.

[50] 2 Kings 4:23; Colossians 2:16.
[51] Exodus 23:14.
[52] Leviticus 23:6, 10.
[53] Leviticus 23:24, 27.
[54] Leviticus 23:2.
[55] Exodus 23:11.
[56] Leviticus 25:10.
[57] The Dave Matthews Band, album released September, 1994.
[58] Virgil's *Georgics*, Book 3, lines 284-285. This work was likely produced in 29 BC.

Chapter 17
A Hut or a Palace?

WHAT REALLY MATTERS MOST IN LIFE?

Very often in Western culture, home is associated with the physical structure in which a family dwells. Families are judged and even judge themselves by the quality of their domicile. Those who live in mansions or palaces are thought to be the most successful families. They are imagined to have the "good life." Indeed, the focus of families can become increasingly competitive, the "keeping-up-with-the-Joneses" syndrome. Instead of serving a utilitarian purpose, houses have become badges of success or the lack thereof.

FALSE GODS AND MISPLACED PRIORITIES

Like some ancient peoples, many modern societies worship the gods of materialism and pleasure. Individuals and families are judged more by the quantity of their possessions than by the quality of their character. The good life is measured by hedonism's standards for *joie de vivre*. Madison Avenue magnates and mavens blast everyone continually with the secret to success, which everyone knows is simply purchasing and possessing the one indispensable thing or enjoying the one pleasure that is currently being advertised and promoted.

This subtle ploy causes extraordinary time, energy, and re-sources that could have been expended upon family relation-ships to be wasted on material things that more often than not rapidly become expendable. Yesterday's must-have treasure is today's yard-sale junk. Indeed, because of planned obsolescence, most consumer products are already outdated when they are purchased. Dictums like "A woman's place is in the mall" and "The only difference between men and boys is the price of their toys" have, therefore, become mantras for today's materialistic, hedonistic societies. The distraction is so subtle that it is often untreatable. What makes most people feel good about themselves is usually either an external status symbol or a momentary pleasure.

How is a Christian family to escape being consumed in this Venus fly-trap of commercialism and hedonism? How can one get off the treadmill of endless and mindless efforts to match one's neighbor with the accoutrements of success? How can a family focus on the home and not on the house? How can a house be a temple of blessing and inclusion rather than a castle of invulnerability and exclusion? There is an answer, and, as usual, that answer is in the Bible!

God has long had a powerful solution to this dilemma in his system of praise, worship, and service that came to be called Judaism. It dates back over 35 centuries to the time when he established a constitution for his family, the Israelites. After God had liberated the family of Jacob from Egyptian bondage, he established a liturgical order for annual holy days and festivals that would help his people remember his deliverance and their appropriate relationship with him. These were to be divine ap-pointments on God's calendar for pre-set times when he would meet with his people and they would meet with one another.

God's appointment calendar began with Passover,[1] proceeded through Pentecost,[2] and concluded with Tabernacles.[3] God said, "These are my appointments."[4] Since Israel was predominantly an agrarian society, God ordained festivals at the beginning, in the middle, and at the end of the harvest season to remind his people that their existence as families, as well as a social and political entity, was wholly dependent upon his sovereign act of deliverance and upon his continuing provision for their sustenance.

God's system was designed to help the Israelites escape the siren song of self-sufficiency that would attempt to draw them away from dependence upon God. If they maintained his celebration system, they would have constant reminders that their identity was not in the things they possessed nor in the power they wielded but in their relationship with God. Each Israelite was to celebrate the Passover by declaring that he himself had been a slave in Egypt and that he, not just his ancestors, was personally delivered by God's hand.[5] He was to see himself as having stood at Sinai on Pentecost, receiving God's Torah of instructions and guidelines for life.[6] He was to see himself as the recipient of God's bounty in the midst of the most abject of circumstances possible. At Tabernacles, he was to understand that he himself had lived in flimsy tents on the way to the land of milk and honey.

THE SUKKAH EXPERIENCE

During the celebration of the Festival of Tabernacles at the end of the year, the Jewish people were commanded to construct huts outside their houses and to dwell in those minimalist, temporary shelters for an entire week. The hut that each family was to build was called in Hebrew a *sukkah*. From this term came the most prominent name of the autumnal festival, *Sukkot* (Tabernacles or Booths, also called the Festival of Ingathering).

Now, this was just the opposite of what human reason would have established for a fall festival. One would think that God would have had his people gather in ornate temples, dress in finery, surround themselves with symbols of bounty, and really celebrate the "good life" by flitting from party to party and reveling in wine, gourmet food, and sexual dalliance—precisely the experiences prescribed for the autumnal fertility rites of pagan idolatry. What better way to celebrate a beneficent God than to revel in the symbols of his bounty! Even today, some might think a true fall festival should honor excess and pay homage to pleasure.

For Israel, however, it was just the opposite: "Build yourself a bare minimalist structure, and live in it for a week," God commanded. Irrational? No, supra-rational! This command did not stand in human rationality; it rested on the infinite understanding of the Almighty which transcends human reason.[7] By this commandment, God ensured that the focus of his people would not be on things but on their God and on their families. Things did not sustain their existence. God did! Their most important possessions were not their houses, lands, or material resources. It was God and the families he had given them. They were not fixated on things. They were focused on relationships!

For the Jews, celebrating the concluding festival of the liturgical year was a constant reminder of the transient nature of human existence. They knew that life is fragile and filled with uncertainty. Solomon lamented the fact that everything under the sun is vanity because no one can take anything with him when he dies.[8] Even in the first century of the Christian experience, James observed that life is like a vapor that vanishes into thin air.[9] God wanted his people to be reminded of the fragility of life. Because God built such a reminder into their calendar to remind his people of life's evanescence it was easier for them to maintain their focus on the priorities of life. In his wisdom, God provided a yearly reminder of these truths for those who are observant of his system of worship.

Human tragedies underscore what is really important, but God's people did not wait for tragedy. They were reminded yearly, monthly, weekly, and daily! But especially at the fall festival of Tabernacles, they were given a vivid reminder of the nature of human existence. The huts that they built and lived in for a week each year were an unforgettable reminder. These flimsy structures bore witness to the truth that those who take God's commandment literally reap the benefit of wisdom gained from the *sukkah* experience.

The *sukkah* also reminded Israel of the unpredictability of physical structures that can be obliterated in a moment's time in cataclysmic natural disasters like storm, flood, fire, or earth-quake, or can be lost virtually overnight in the midst of the vicissitudes of economic upheavals. Yesterday's castle is tomorrow's archaeological ruin. Only one thing in life is more certain than the proverbial "death and taxes" and that is God and his all-sufficient provision for his children. The minimalist hut called the *sukkah* reinforced to the Israelites that structures which seem secure can literally evaporate into thin air.

What is really important in life? What are the things that one can take with him beyond the grave or that can survive him in the future? The material objects deemed so important that family relationships and moral and ethical standards are sacri-ficed in order to gain them end up in estate sales and are fodder for family arguments and divisions after one dies. On the other hand, family relationships are the treasures that endure even beyond the grave. Children and grandchildren are one's ticket to the future. It is only through them that the living are able to propel their values and memories into the future.[10]

When one eats, sleeps, and engages in family life in a hut for a week each year, a golden opportunity is created to sort out priorities and maintain focus. The hut experience is good for humankind. It reflects the truth of where humans could be if it were not for God's bountiful provision. Hut living reinforces thankfulness for what God has provided and minimizes the human tendency towards violating the tenth commandment of the Decalogue—the prohibition against covetousness. All huts are the same—huts. None has an imposing façade or an ornate interior, even thought they are often decorated elaborately. *Sukkot,* therefore, is a great equalizer when all people experience their humanity and God's provision on the same level.

Amazingly, the Jewish people have never considered their *sukkah* experience to be a burden. They have viewed Tabernacles as the greatest of all biblical festivals, "The Feast" and have called it the "Season of our Joy," the most wonderful festival of the year. *Sukkot* is also believed to be a universal celebration that bids all humankind, both Jew and Gentile, to come together and rejoice in the bounty of God's blessings and to celebrate the joy of freedom. Indeed, in the Age to Come, Zechariah 14 declares that Tabernacles will be celebrated by all the peoples of the earth.

The festival seasons of Scripture were also special times for opening the family temple to the strangers, orphans, widows, and the poor. This exercise protected the Jewish family temple from becoming introverted, elitist, and exclusive. God specifically commanded it: "You shall rejoice in your festival, with your son and daughter . . . the stranger, the fatherless and the widow in your communities."[11] The great Talmudist Moses Maimonides expanded this concept: "One who locks the doors to his courtyard and eats and drinks with his wife and children, without giving anything . . . to the poor and bitter in soul—his meal is not 'the joy of the commandment,' but the joy of his stomach. . . . Rejoicing of this kind is a disgrace."[12] Tabernacles is for sharing the grace of God and the love of family, friends, and even strangers.

A CHRISTIAN FESTIVAL OF TABERNACLES

Jesus himself celebrated this integral part of his biblical heritage. On the last great day of the Festival of Tabernacles, he stood up in the temple complex and proclaimed, "If anyone is thirsty, let him come to me and drink."[13] His offer no doubt coincided with the water libation that was an essential part of the *Sukkot* experience for the corporate Jewish community when the High Priest took water from the Pool of Siloam and poured it out on the altar of the temple in expectation of the coming rains that would produce the harvests in the land of Israel. At this time, Jerusalem echoed with shouts of *"Hoshanah!"* ("God save us!"), which was a form of prayer saying, "God make it rain," but was also an exclamation of praise to the coming King. These are the same shouts of praise that will again echo in Jerusalem when the King of kings establishes his dominion over all the earth in the Messianic Age.

In ancient Israel, there was profound, ecstatic worship in the Temple and a liturgical order for the community's interaction. Blazing menorahs, spectacular dancing, and solemn ritual brought excitement to Jerusalem. Though it had important corporate significance, the Tabernacles experience, like virtually every other worship exercise in Judaism, was a family affair. The focus was on the family hut, with each family celebrating its dependence upon God. Even today, among the Jewish people, the focus of *Sukkot* continues to remain on the family.

The *sukkah* experience that the Israelites enjoyed and that the Jews to this day celebrate can also be shared in the Christian community. Corporate worship exercises can be carried out to encourage believers to rejoice in God's bounty and provision for his children. This is a good time to celebrate salvation history as it related to Israel's *Sukkot* celebrations and to rejoice in the eschatological dimensions of Tabernacles that point to the coming of the Messiah to establish God's dominion over the earth.[13] Corporate worship can be as eventful and celebratory as it was in ancient Israel and as it has been among the Jewish people through the centuries until the present day.

The focus of the Christian Tabernacles celebration should,

however, be on the family and those who are welcomed into its sanctuary, not just on a public corporate demonstration. Christian families can also profit from God's instructions to their ancient Israelite forbears. They can build huts outside their houses, gather in them as family units, and remember that life on earth is only temporary and that eternal bliss in the presence of God awaits those who are faithful to his will. Spending a few nights in a hut will underscore the bounty that the family enjoys and will help each member to understand that what is important in his life is not possessions but relationships, both with God, with family, and with community.

For a family that is wholly dependent upon the clergy for all its worship experiences, the *Sukkot* experience may seem daunting, even impossible. "Why can't the pastor build a hut as a model so we can see it and get the idea and go home?" they might moan, or they might reason, "Why can't we just look at a poster of the Israelites' huts and get the lesson from that?" Those accustomed to performance-based, audience-based religion might think this is the only way they can profit from the Tabernacles lesson. But, there is much more for those who say to themselves, "Let's just try God's idea and see what it does for us!"

For those who have restored the family temple to their personal experience, the Tabernacles experience is a natural expression of their already-existing family worship agenda. If God said it, it must be profitable. Indeed, God's Word works! The only thing that is needed is people to have enough faith in God to do what he said. When autumn comes and the Tabernacles season approaches, go ahead and build your own *sukkah* outside your home. What the neighbors think doesn't matter. In fact, if you do it right, you may just get an opportunity to witness to your faith and share with them the value of this annual biblical opportunity to reaffirm your family priorities.

Whatever you have been doing in your home throughout the year when you engage in family time for social interconnectivity, you can do in your hut. What you have done in studying God's Word together can become a fresh and invigorating experience when you do it in your hut. What you have been doing in praying and worshipping together can be powerfully strengthened as you peer through the branches of the flimsy shelter, view the stars, and, with Israel of old, envision the coming of the Messiah. You can even pretend with your children that you are on the wilderness journey, bound for the Promised Land—and, indeed, this life is but a journey much like Israel's wilderness expereience, only toward the Age to Come, the Messianic Era.

You can celebrate all of God's festivals in the context of your family temple. Just as the father or head of household in ancient Israel killed the lamb and led his family in the Passover celebration, you can lead your family in the yearly Passover by honoring the Paschal Lamb who was slain from the foundation of the world and who redeemed humanity from sin and death. Likewise, you can lead your family in celebrating God's provision of his Word at Sinai and his Spirit at Zion as you memorialize Pentecost, imagining that you, too, heard God's thundering voice proclaim his commandments and that you likewise can experience anew the infilling of the Holy Spirit. Finally, you can lead your family in celebrating the festival of festivals, the feast of joy, Tabernacles. And you can do it in your own family temple that you have moved from the security of your home into the flimsy, temporary hut that God instructed.

CONSTRUCTING YOUR OWN FAMILY SUKKAH

Among the Jewish people, it is considered a *mitzvah* (a good deed in fulfillment of a divine commandment) to build one's own *sukkah* (hut). While this was a part of God's commandment to Israel, it is also a good object lesson for Christian families.

You can share with the Jewish people the joy of delighting to fulfill God's instructions[15] and thereby actually find yourself "delighting in the Lord.[16]

The Feast of Tabernacles comes in the fall of the year (usually in late September or early October). If you want to have your celebration coincide with that of the Jewish people, consult a Jewish calendar for the exact time or simply enter "Tabernacles date" in your computer or smart phone search engine. The Festival of Tabernacles is celebrated for eight days from Tishri 15-23 on the Jewish calendar.

**A *Sukkah* (Hut) for the
Feast of Tabernacles**

Start your plans a few weeks before the time comes to build. You will need to devise a plan for the size and the materials you will need. The *sukkah* can be any size as long as it is large enough to sit inside. A good, practical size is around seven feet in length, width, and height.

Since the *sukkah* is meant to be a temporary hut, you can use materials that are lightweight and easy to handle. It is best to use four posts (2 x 2's are fine) for the corners. Four additional poles can be used for the roof. All of these poles need to be around eight feet in length.

Corner posts can be anchored as uprights in the holes of concrete blocks or with stacked bricks or other material placed strategically on the ground. Make sure that the corner posts are securely anchored so that they will remain upright. The four 2 x 2's that form the beams for the top perimeter of the *sukkah* can be nailed or screwed together and then attached to the tops of the four 2 x 2 corner posts. Make sure that the corner posts and the beams are securely fastened to each other to ensure that the structure is sound. Once the frame is constructed, use cloth or other materials including canvas, cane matting, cardboard, or thin plywood to cover three of the sides of your *sukkah*. (An existing building wall may serve as one of the sides.) Attach a bed sheet or similar material on a wire track at the top of the fourth side that you want to use as an entrance.

Finally, in order to cover the roof of your *sukkah*, you will need small boards capable of supporting light tree branches (1 x 2's are fine). Then, on top you can place palm or other tree branches, being careful to leave openings so that while sitting in the *sukkah* at night you can still see the stars. This further underscores the temporary nature of the structure and gives you the opportunity to visualize the coming of the Messiah in the clouds of the heavens.

You can furnish your *sukkah* to your own taste, with table and chairs or other items. You can use pictures or other decorative items. Fruit can be hung from the ceiling to emphasize the festive Tabernacles season. You should certainly involve your children in the construction and decoration of your *sukkah*. This is an excellent time for them to learn the process and share in the excitement with their own creativity.

After you have constructed your *sukkah*, you can assemble family and friends in this "tabernacle" for fellowship, study, prayer, and worship. Try having a meal together in the *sukkah*. You might even want to spend a night there. If the weather is inclement, be safe and healthy and spend the time in your home; however, if he weather is good, spend some time in this temporary enclosure searching the heavens and expressing your expectation for the coming of the Mesisah.

Above all, remember that God has committed himself to meeting with you and your family and friends at the time of this

divine appointment. Remember also that life is a vapor that soon
passess away, and renew afresh your understanding of the things
in life that are truly important: your personal relationship with
God, your personal relationship with your family, your personal
relationship with other members of the community of believers,
and your personal relatinship with friends and neighbors in the
entire human family. You can celebrate all of these blessings in
the setting of the hut that you have constructed and have made
into your family temple.

[1] Exodus 12:11-48.

[2] Exodus 19:1-23.

[3] Exodus 23:16.

[4] Leviticus 23:2.

[5] Exodus 13:8 teaches: "You shall tell your son on that day, saying, It is because of what the LORD did for me when I came out of Egypt." Deuteronomy 5:15 says, "You shall remember that you were a slave in the land of Egypt, and the LORD your God brought you out of there by a mighty hand." See Joel Lurie Grishaver, *Experiencing the Jewish Holidays* (Los Angeles: Tora Aura Production, 2011), p. 104.

[6] In Deuteronomy 29:14-15, God said, "Neither with you alone do I make this covenant . . . but with him that standeth here with us this day before the LORD our God, and also with him that is not here with us this day." Cf. Midrash *Tanhuma B. Nizzabin*, 8:25b. See Fred N. Reiner, *Standing at Sinai: Sermons and Writings* (Bloomington, IN: AuthorHouse, 2011), p. 173. Also Judith Ochshom and Ellen Cole, *Women's Spirituality, Women's Lives* (Binghamton, NY: The Haworth Press, 1995), p. 74.

[7] 1 Corinthians 2:14.

[8] Ecclesiastes 1:14.

[9] James 4:14.

[10] Psalm 127:4.

[11] Deuteronomy 16:14.

[12] Moses Maimonides, *Mishneh Torah*, "Laws of the Festivals," 6:18.

[13] John 7:37.

[14] Zechariah 14:4, 16-18.

[15] Psalm 1:2; 49:8; 119:174.

[16] Psalm 37:4.

Chapter 18

Restoring the Family Temple

THE CHURCH IS GOING HOME

Much like Solomon's temple, the family temple has suffered destruction both as a conceptual idea and as a practical reality. Something akin to Babylon has overwhelmed this ancient, biblically Hebraic formula, replacing it almost exclusively with corporate sanctuaries and public worship. Now it is time for a restoration to take place akin to that of the time of Ezra and Nehemiah, of Joshua and Zerubbabel, of Haggai and Zechariah.

The home that has for so long been relegated to a position of relative unimportance as a mere social convention must now be restored to the position of honor that it had in biblical times as the family temple. In a day of growing onslaughts against this, the fundamental societal unit, it is imperative that both the Jewish and Christian communities hold up the biblical standard of family identity in the face of the virulent attack of the enemy. The family must be restored as the center for social, educational, and spiritual development. Anything less spells disaster for both church and society at large.

Each family must view its home as a sanctuary, a mini-temple in which all the functions of biblical community life have their beginnings and are fully manifest. This restoration will restore a God-consciousness to both the church and society that will transcend the nominal Christian experience. It will return the family of God to a face-to-face relationship of walking with God, the spiritual experience that predated both Judaism and Christianity. In effect, it will be Eden renewed in the family temple!

For centuries, the Christian home has been dysfunctional in many ways because its original Hebraic foundations have been eroded by influences from Gentile philosophies and religious systems. In recent decades, it has suffered violent attack from secularists bent on redefining the family to accommodate politically correct tolerance for aberrations and perversions. Biblical family roles have been replaced in the public square through insidious, vicious attacks camouflaged as "values-clarification." The all-wise state knows what is best for society, and it inculcates and enforces the official, state-sponsored religion of secular humanism through its school systems, from pre-school to graduate-level college programs, attacking and brainwashing the most vulnerable members of society, the children.

Millions of Christians are now seeking a remedy for this malady. In large part, the church has been unable and perhaps unwilling to lead believers in finding the answer. For some eighteen centuries it has actually contributed to the problem by removing from the home its biblically Hebraic heritage, replacing the biblical focus on the family with programs designed to promote the institutional church. Instead of encouraging lay participation in extra-ecclesial study and worship in the context of the family, the official church centuries ago redefined what it meant to be "church," limiting the first-century biblical roles of the family and subsuming those into the interests of the ecclesio-political institutionalized church.

The major vehicle which made this redefinition of "church" possible was the creation of an enduring distinction between clergy and laity, a false dichotomy that exalted professional clergy to an elevated state of holiness and made them superior to the church constituency. This eventually divided the church into two churches, the *ecclesia clerens* (the teaching church) and the *ecclesia audiens* (the listening church). With this innovation, performance-based Christianity became the official norm. Like their contemporaries who gathered in imposing, grandiose temples to witness the theatre of pagan rites, the laity of the church assembled in ever more magnificent cathedrals to view the spectacle of priestly performance that was increasingly veiled in mystery, further elevating the power and prestige of the clergy.

The result of this gradual shift of emphasis from the home to the church was and remains to this day debilitating to the church body politic. One of its immediate results was the decline of learning in the areas where the church dominated. Learning became almost exclusively the province of the church and its professional clergy. Eventually, the masses became totally illiterate. The masses were even restricted from having access to the Word of God, even upon penalty of death.[1] When the church assumed exclusive rights to worship experiences, the masses no longer worshipped in their homes. Increasingly, the masses became more superstitious and dependent upon occasional "church" experiences for any sense of spirituality.

When renewal movements finally emerged both within and outside the official church, they did not address the real problem that was debilitating the church: the virtual destruction of the family temple. The clergy-laity gap remained intact with only minor adjustments. Church institutions and the clergy continued to be the focus of Christian activity. Spectator Christianity was maintained in one form or another and still remains the dominant form of religious expression in today's church. One needs only to look at the competing billboards of mega-churches or the hype of the "electronic church" to see that spectator Christianity continues to be the norm.

GOING BACK IN ORDER TO GO FORWARD

Individuals who have a passion for more than the nominal Christian experience have grown restless in the face of ecclesiastical unresponsiveness to their need for intimacy with God. Increasingly, they are turning to small groups and are meeting in homes for fellowship, study, and worship. Most of these groups represent the church's very best talent, its most dedicated members. They are searching for a spiritual reality that will build faith in their hearts and in their homes. Because they have not found answers in traditional institutional structures, believers have begun to assume responsibility for their own spiritual growth. The result has been the emergence of an indigenous home-church movement.

Returning the focus of Christian experience to the home has created a need for community fellowship and corporate worship experiences of like-minded people. The movement back to the family is crying out for leadership that encourages family worship and study while providing biblically mandated opportunities for fellowship, study, and worship in the context of community. In reality, the church should be facilitating this refocus on the home and the family, restoring both to biblical perspectives. Church leaders should come to understand themselves as facilitators for individuals and families, equipping believers for works of ministry in every arena of life.[2]

A rethinking of both the church and the family must be undertaken if both are to survive the onslaught of secularism's unrelenting onslaught. It is time for in-depth analysis of theology's most neglected area of investigation: ecclesiology (the study of the church). What constitutes the church? How does it function? What is its purpose? These are issues that theologians and church leaders around the world must face head on. Questions of what constitutes worship, fellowship, and service must also be answered. In short, Christianity must reexamine itself from within before it crumbles from within, and it must redefine itself in terms of its original, inherent ideal.

A return to the biblical models in which Jesus and the apostles lived their lives and expressed their devotion to the heavenly Father will empower the church to experience the profound growth and the phenomenal power that it enjoyed in its earliest formative days. The Lord will add to the church daily in ever-increasing numbers when it continues to model its earliest daily dynamic, having fellowship, teaching, and prayers, breaking bread from house to house.

While the family temple will never replace the corporate worshipping community, if encouraged to function in biblically Hebraic order, the home church will cause the corporate community of believers to experience explosive growth. Traditional high levels of recidivism among new converts to Christianity will be negated by returning the focus for discipleship and maturity to the family temple when family and then small groups of extended family and friends meet for fellowship, study, and worship. When the home is the locus for spiritual growth, everyone has a sphere of accountability, and the corporate community grows both qualitatively and quantitatively.

The Holistic Home

For far too long, the lives of Christians, both individuals and families, have been separated, bifurcated into two hemispheres, the spiritual and the secular. Influenced by neo-Platonism and residues of Gnosticism,[3] the church has reinforced this perspective by removing spiritual leadership from the home and assigning it almost exclusively to the church. This application of Greek dualism has encouraged individuals and families to live in two realms, one spiritual, the other secular. More often than not, the spiritual sphere for them has been the church and the experiences they share periodically in church worship centers. The home, consequently, has generally been left by default in the secular domain. This perspective has made the home easy prey for the entertainment industry and has allowed secularism to diminish and eliminate spiritual exercises from its confines.

When one bypasses the Americanization, Europeanization, Latinization, and Hellenization of Christianity and returns to the church's Hebraic foundations, dualism is no longer an option. Life cannot be dichotomized to allow different lifestyles and ethics in spiritual and secular realms. For the Hebrews, everything was theological and spiritual. As Marvin Wilson notes, ". . . the Hebrews made no distinction between the sacred and the secular areas of life. . . . They see all of life as a unity."[4] From the mundane to the sublime, all aspects of life were to be lived under the purview of God's instructions. Everything was to be done to the glory of God.[5]

Hebraic holism does not permit areas of life to be off limits for God's instructions and proper, ethical conduct. The commandments of God apply in the home just as they apply in the church. They are just as viable in the public square and in the world of commerce as they are in the church. A family temple is a sure cure for domestic violence, for how can one dare to manifest destructive behavior if the home is also recognized as a house of God?

When all of life is lived for God, the spiritual begins in the individual heart, then extends to the family, and finally reaches fullest flower in community. What is biblically mandated to be done in the corporate community of believers must first be done in individual hearts and then in individual families. Instead of a divisive dualism that walls off the spiritual dimensions of their lives from the dominant secular realm, believers experience a healthy holism. They are working in partnership with God in the Hebraic process of *tikkun olam*[6] (restoration of the world), beginning with themselves, then with their families, and finally with their communities and the world. They are, like Adam, "keepers of the garden"—in this case, the sanctuary of their own home.[7]

Impacting community and the world begins at home when the family temple opens its sacred assembly to friends and extended family and even to strangers. Like Sarah's tent, the family temple is a place for Hebraic hospitality. Bringing others into the sanctuary keeps it from becoming exclusive and elitist, from being introverted, turned in on itself and vulnerable to aberrant, cultic devices. It adds strength from the blessing that others have to impart into the family and from the blessing that the family bestows upon others.

This is not merely an idyllic, utopian view of family. It is an opportunity to believe in and aspire to the ideal while experiencing and dealing with the real. It is retreating into the sanctuary of God's instructions while facing the difficulties in life that result from fallen humanity. It is assuming responsibility for individual and family growth while maintaining respect for the input of divinely appointed community spiritual leaders. It is an effort to bring heaven to earth by involving God in every aspect of human existence.

CALLING TIME OUT

Wise Christians are learning to call time out. Enough is enough! It is time to retreat into the sanctuary of loving, affirming relationships. Once the family temple is built and fortified—or is simply recognized—as a place of refuge and strength that it was always designed to be, it is accessible to every member of the family. All one needs to do is to call time. When set times for family interaction have been established, quality time that has seemed so fleeting and unachievable becomes available and sufficient. If pressures mount or situations arise that do not conform to the family appointment calendar, one can call time out and retreat into the sanctuary for communion with God and family that brings renewal and fresh resolve to face life's challenges.

Wise Christian leaders are even calling time out from the excessive programs that have been devised to keep individuals and families involved in the church. They are learning to multiply the effectiveness of their ministries by training and equipping heads of households who can, in turn, replicate the teaching and worship in their own homes, thereby multiplying and strengthening the church exponentially. Rather than making involvement in church programs almost a requisite of salvation, they are insisting that families create time sanctuaries for their families and fully realize the blessings of God upon their homes.

Translocal leaders of the Christian community are also calling time out to rethink traditional Christianity and to stop the rat race of doing the same things over and over again. Insanity has been defined as continuing to do the same things that one has been doing all the while expecting a different outcome. If the results that the church is achieving are not acceptable—and they are not—it is time for spiritual leaders to yell, "Time out!" Leaders need to take a sabbatical for reflection and renewal on the task of restoring and strengthening the church's fundamental and founding unit, the family temple.

It is also time for leaders to make appointments to consider how the old paths wherein is the good way can be restored.[8] It is time for church leaders to give careful consideration to rebuilding the holy city's walls, to closing up the breaches made by unrelenting attacks from the enemy.[9] Historical breaches made by ecclesiastical potentates and their bureaucracies must be restored. Present breaches by secular humanism must be recognized and repaired. It is time to restore the tent of David that has fallen into such disarray.[10] It is time to renew the faith once delivered to the saints.[11]

GOING HOME

The growing need for sanctuary in a world gone mad is driving more and more people into the one environment that they have the potential to control, their own homes. As societal insanity, fueled by moral bankruptcy, increasingly breeds socio-paths and psychopaths bent upon indiscriminate violence and seeks to suppress individual freedoms for religious expression, parents feel the need to cordon off space and erect barricades against perversion and emotional and physical threats. They are retreating with their children to the enduring sanctuary of the family temple.

There is rarely a more gratifying moment than being able to go back home after a long excursion to a distant place. Likewise, it is satisfying and spiritually rewarding to go back to the place where the church and the synagogue began, the family temple. What began in a garden home and was more fully manifest in the tent of a family of faith reached full manifestation in the congregation of Israel. What was initiated in Jewish homes in Babylon was fully realized in the diverse and spiritually enriching synagogal experiences in both Judaea and the diaspora. What started in Jewish Christian homes during the Roman occupation came to full flower in the congregations of Christ throughout the world. Everything started with the family temple.

If the family temple is where both Judaism and Christianity had their origins, then it would seem that restoring biblically Hebraic concepts for family and home will surely bring renewal and health to modern manifestations of the family, the syna-gogue, and the church. Understanding that the home is a *mikdash me'at* (a temple in miniature) complete with a family altar and a functioning priesthood will revolutionize the life and ministry of the church, bringing a renewed and enduring vitality that will not be eroded by the short attention span of the modern mind. Christians are coming to understand what is truly important in life: God and family. Increasing numbers are embracing the roots of Christian faith that are anchored deep in the soil of biblical Judaism. To growing numbers of believers, rediscovering the Hebraic foundations of Christian faith is becoming a golden key that for them unlocks the treasures of Holy Scripture and enriches their lives.

The institution of the church is also headed home. In a quest for orthodoxy, some are stopping at Canterbury, Geneva, Wittenburg, Rome, or Constantinople. Many, however, are determined to go all the way back home—to Jerusalem and the Hebraic roots of their faith. When they make the determined climb to "go up to Jerusalem"[12] and when they reach the lofty heights of that city of gold, they experience that swell of emotion and the sigh of satisfaction that says, "I'm home!" And so they are—home where the Christian church had its beginnings; home where the faith destined for all nations began its trek around the world; home where they can relax and enjoy the contentment of personal and family growth—emotionally, intellectually, and spiritually.

Now is the time for believers everywhere to follow the leading of the Holy Spirit to go back home. It is time to restore the one faith for all peoples, the Hebraic heritage of the prophets and sages of Israel and of Jesus and the apostles of the church. Nowhere is this restoration more important than in the Christian home and family. It is time to stop bemoaning the onslaught of human and demonic forces against the Christian faith and start restoring health and vitality to the faith's most fundamental unit, the family. It is time to restore the family temple. Men and women of vision are now declaring without reservation, "As for me and my house, we will serve the Lord,"[13] and, at long last, the church is, indeed, going home—back to the family temple!

[1] A prime example was William Tyndale who dared to produce the Scriptures in the English language and who as a result was executed by strangulation and had his body burned at the stake in 1636. Tyndale said this of the determined effort of the Roman Catholic Church to keep the Scriptures from the common people: "In the universities they have ordained that no man shall look on the scripture, until he be noselled [nursed] in heathen learning eight or nine years, and armed with false principles; with which he is clean shut out of the understanding of the scripture." See William Tyndale, *Expositions and Notes on Sundry Portions of the Holy Scriptures, Together with the Practice of Prelates,* Henry Walter, ed. (Cambridge: Cambridge University Press, 1849), p. 291.

[2] Ephesians 4:11-12.

[3] Platonic and Gnostic dualism teaches that the material is evil while the spiritual is good. The Bible teaches no such bifurcation, clearly declaring that everything was created by God. While anything can be used for evil, nothing is "unclean of itself" (Romans 14:14).

[4] Marvin R. Wilson, *Our Father Abraham: Jewish Roots of the Christian Faith* (Grand Rapids, MI: Wm. B. Eerdmans Publishing Co., 1989), p. 156.

[5] 1 Corinthians 10:31.

[6] The Jewish concept of *tikkun olam* suggests that God always works in partnership with humans in the effort to renew and restore the world to its original design. See Elliot N. Dorff and Cory Wilson, *The Jewish Approach to Repairing the World (Tikkun Olam): A Brief Introduction for Christians* (Woodstock, VT: Jewish Lights Publications, 2008). Also, David Shatz, Chaim Isaac Waxman, and Nathan J. Diament, *Tikkun Olam: Social Responsibility in Jewish Thought and Law* (Jason Aronson Publishing, 1997), p. 1, which rightly connects the ultimate fulfillment of *tikkun olam* with the messianic age but notes that the principles apply in every era.

[7] Genesis 2:15.

[8] Jeremiah 6:16.

[9] Amos 9:11.

[10] Acts 15:15-16.

[11] Jude 1:3.

[12] Isaiah 2:3.

[13] Joshua 24:15.

Index

BOOKS BY DR. JOHN D. GARR

God and Women establishes the fact God's image is manifest in both women and men. As you read this book, will be amazed at what the Bible really says about women as God made them.

Bless You! is a thorough study of the biblical blessing that will help you understand what God had in mind when he commanded that his own blessing be placed on his children forever.

Coequal and Counterbalanced represents serious scholarship on the way in which God created women and men to manifest perfectly counterbalanced and complementary mutuality.

Passover: The Festival of Redemption studies the first and foremost festival in Scripture that was the foundation both of Judaism with the Exodus and of Christianity with the Calvary event.

Feminine by Design is a comprehensive study of the way in which God fashioned woman to reflect perfect femininity that is manifest through beauty, modesty, nurture, relationality, and freedom.

The Hem of His Garment examines the touching story of a dying woman who was healed by touching Jesus, a story that will help you to understand what faith in God's Word will do for you.

Blessings for Family and Friends is a stunningly beautiful gift book that provides you with a wide range of templates for biblical blessings which will revolutionize and enhance your family life.

God's Lamp, Man's Light is a thorough study of the only biblical symbol that God himself designed. You will be blessed by the mysteries that are contained in the design of the menorah.

Our Lost Legacy analyzes the historical separation of the Christian church from the original Hebraic foundations of the faith of Jesus and the apostles, and it calls for a restoration of those foundations.

Living Emblems evaluates the ancient biblical symbols of faith that unveil profound truths from God's Word while serving as pictures that reveal the Messiahship of the Lord Jesus.

Order from:

HEBRAIC CHRISTIAN GLOBAL COMMUNITY
P. O. Box 421218, Atlanta, Georgia 30342, U.S.A.

www.HebraicCommunity.org

HEBRAIC HERITAGE

C H R I S T I A N   C E N T E R

Hebraic Heritage Christian Center is an institution of higher education that is dedicated to the vision of restoring a Hebraic model for Christian education. A consortium of scholars, spiritual leaders, and business persons, the Center features a continually developing curriculum in which each course of study is firmly anchored in the Hebrew foundations of the Christian faith.

The Hebraic Heritage Christian Center vision combines both the ancient and the most modern in an educational program that conveys knowledge, understanding, and wisdom to a world-wide student population. The Center seeks to restore the foundations of original Christianity in order to equip its students with historically accurate, theologically sound understanding of the biblical faith that Jesus and the apostles instituted and practiced. At the same time the Center endeavors to implement the finest in innovative, cutting-edge technology in a distance-learning program that delivers its user-friendly courses by the Internet.

Among the wide range of services and products that Hebraic Heritage Christian Center offers are the publications of Hebraic Heritage Press. These are delivered both in traditional print media as well as in electronic media to serve both the Center's student population and the general public with inspiring and challenging materials that have been developed by the Center's team of scholars.

Those who are interested in sharing in the development of Hebraic Heritage Christian Center and its commitment to restoring the Jewish roots of the Christian faith are invited to join the Founders' Club, people who support this team of scholars and leaders by becoming co-founders of this institution. Many opportunities for endowments are also available to those who wish to create a lasting memorial to the cause of Christian renewal and Christian-Jewish rapprochement.

HEBRAIC HERITAGE CHRISTIAN CENTER
P. O. Box 450848
Atlanta, GA 31145-0848
www.HebraicCenter.org

Get Your <u>Free</u> Copy

of

The Magazine That's Restoring the Biblically Hebraic Heritage to Christian Believers Around the World

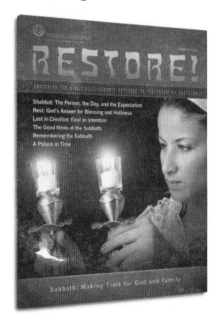

Restore! is the exciting journal that's. . .

✡ *helping Christians around the world to restore the Jewish roots of their faith in Jesus Christ.*

✡ *fighting against Judaeophobia, anti-Judaism, and anti-Semitism in the Christian church.*

✡ *encouraging Christians to support the international Jewish community and the nation of Israel.*

✡ *promoting unity (cohesiveness in the midst of diversity) within the universal body of Christ.*

HERE'S WHAT SOME OF OUR READERS ARE SAYING ABOUT *Restore!*

"I consider *Restore!* to be the best magazine on the restoration of Jewish roots because of its quality of presentation of the various topics, its scholarly articles, and most important, the strengthening of our faith that results the articles."—Michael Katritsis, Athens, Greece.

"*Restore!* is the best magazine I have ever read, the only one which I have read cover to cover."—Colyn King, Levin, New Zealand.

"*Restore!* is an inspiration both in its quality and the profundity of its contents."—Jorge Robles Olarte, Medellin, Columbia.

Restore!

Hebraic Christian Global Community

P. O. Box 421218
Atlanta, GA 30342